DECORATIVE SEWING
for the home

DECORATIVE SEWING
for the home

OVER 40 CREATIVE SOFT FURNISHING PROJECTS

100 IDEES

CONRAN OCTOPUS

First published in 1991 by
Conran Octopus Limited
37 Shelton Street
London WC2H 9HN

ISBN 1 85029 323 6

British Library Cataloguing in Publication Data
Decorative sewing for the home.
1. Sewing
I. 100 Idées
646.21

Typeset by SX Composing Limited & The Creative Text Partnership
Printed in Hong Kong

CONTENTS

CONTENTS

CONTENTS

QUILTING   85

CONTENTS

INTRODUCTION

This stunning collection of patterns takes home sewing into a whole new dimension. It features original French designs which use decorative sewing techniques in unexpected and inventive ways, offering a wonderful source of inspiration to all those who like their homes to reflect their personalities and who delight in the individuality that unusual hand-made soft furnishings give to any room.

As the emphasis is on the creative aspect of sewing, the needlework skills of appliqué, quilting and patchwork are used to superb effect in both traditional and innovative ways. These crafts, although they may appear to require specialist skills, are all based on straightforward sewing techniques which anyone who enjoys using a needle or a sewing machine can tackle.

Some items can be run up in no time if you want quick results – for example, the dramatic bedroom set on page 28. Others, such as the Mexican-style appliqué cushions on page 72 or the crazy patchwork quilt on page 118, will provide many hours of pleasure if you prefer to relax with some hand sewing. For quilting enthusiasts there are impressive dinosaur sleeping bags, realistic enough to delight your children, and a magnificent white wall hanging with an antique look.

In the Basic Essentials sections you will find helpful information about enlarging and transferring designs, working seams and bindings and using hand stitches. The techniques used in appliqué, quilting and patchwork are also described. And with the simple step-by-step instructions and diagrams throughout the book, even beginners will feel confident about trying the patterns.

So whether your home is traditional or modern, and whether you want to create an heirloom, find a witty way to decorate a tablecloth or simply give your cushions an interesting new lease of life, DECORATIVE SEWING FOR THE HOME will give you all the ideas you will need for a long time.

DECORATIVE SEWING

BASIC ESSENTIALS

The patterns in this section are easy to use if you follow the methods for enlarging and transferring designs given below. Throughout, plain seams are used unless otherwise stated.

ENLARGING A DESIGN

If the design is already on a square grid, simply copy it, square for square, onto a grid of the correct finished size. Dressmakers' pattern paper can be used for this or, for smaller designs, ordinary graph paper. The most accurate way to copy is to mark each place where the lines of the design cross the lines of the large grid and then to join up these marks.

If the design in the book is not already on a grid, simply draw a squared grid on tracing paper, stick this over the image which you wish to copy, using masking tape at the corners, then trace off the image and enlarge it as already described.

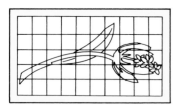

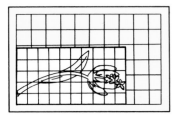

TRANSFERRING A DESIGN

Use dressmakers' carbon paper, which is available in different colours. Stick the fabric to a flat surface, using strips of masking tape at the corners. If the fabric is too large to be stuck to the surface, pin the relevant portion in place with drawing pins. Make a tracing of the design and tape

this over the fabric, then slip the carbon paper face down between the fabric and the tracing. Trace the design.

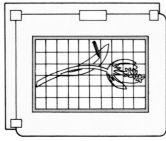

SEAMS

Plain seam

Place the two fabric pieces with right sides together, raw edges level; pin and stitch together 1.5cm (⅝in) from the raw edges. Work a few stitches in reverse at each end of the seam to secure the threads.

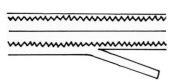

The simplest method of neatening the seam allowance edges is by zigzag stitching on a sewing-machine. Use a short, narrow stitch worked slightly in from the raw edge. If the fabric has a tendency to fray use a larger stitch and work over the raw edge. Where the fabric is fine turn under the raw edge and either zigzag stitch or straight stitch. If neatening by hand, oversew the raw edges: work from left to right, taking the thread diagonally over the edge and keeping the stitches about 3mm (⅛in) apart. If the fabric tends to fray, work a row of straight stitching first, then oversew over the edge. If the fabric is very heavy simply pink the edges using a pair of pinking shears.

Flat fell seam

This is a self-neatening seam that is very strong and distinctive. Place the two fabric pieces with right sides together and raw edges level; pin and stitch together 1.5cm (⅝in) from the raw edges. Press the seam allowance to one side. Trim down the lower seam allowance to 6mm (¼in). Fold the upper seam allowance over, enclosing the lower seam allowance. Press the folded allowance flat against the fabric; pin and stitch close to the folded edge.

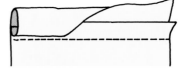

French seam

This is a self-neatening seam. Place the two fabric pieces with wrong sides together; pin and stitch 6mm (¼in) from the raw edges. Press the seam open. Refold with right sides together; pin and stitch 1cm (⅜in) from the seamed edge.

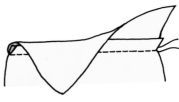

FASTENINGS

How to insert a zip

Pin and tack the seam into which the zip is to be inserted. Stitch in from each, or from one, end of the seam, leaving an opening the same length as the zip. Press the

tacked seam open. Place the zip face down over the seam allowances with the bottom stop 3mm (⅛in) beyond the tacking at one side and with the teeth centred over the tacked seam. Tack in place through all layers 6mm (¼in) on either side of the

teeth. Turn to the right side. Stitch the zip in place using a zipper foot on the sewing-machine or backstitch by hand, following the tacking lines at the sides and pivoting the stitching at the bottom corners or at both ends.

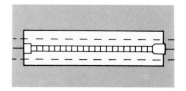

Stitched buttonholes

Mark the buttonhole length the same diameter as the button. Tack all round the buttonhole position and then cut along the marked buttonhole line, along a single thread of fabric, through all layers. Oversew the cut edges with small stitches. Either using buttonhole thread or ordinary sewing thread, secure the thread inside the two fabrics and work along the slit in buttonhole stitch, working a straight bar of stitches at the end. Repeat along the opposite side and end.

BIAS STRIPS

To cut the fabric on the bias fold the fabric so that the selvedge (warp threads) lies exactly parallel to the weft threads. The fold formed is the true cross. Cut along the fold and then cut the bias strips parallel to this edge.

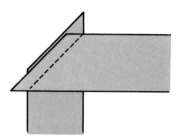

Mark off the strips using pins or a marking pen and cut out. To join strips together, place two strips with right sides together on the straight of grain, as shown, and stitch together taking 6mm (¼in) seams. Trim off points level with side edges and press seam open.

MITRING THE CORNERS

Mitring a fabric band

Fold the fabric band in half lengthways. At one short end, fold the corners back to meet at the folded edge and press. Cut along the diagonal fold lines. Repeat at opposite end of strip so the point is facing in the opposite direction. Repeat with all strips. Unfold two adjoining

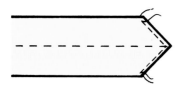

strips and place with right sides together and pointed ends matching. Pin and stitch the end, beginning and ending the stitching 1.5cm (⅝in) from either end of the seam. Trim and turn to the right side, refolding the strip in half. Repeat, to form each mitred corner. Place one edge to main piece with right sides together; pin and stitch. Turn under remaining edge of band. Slipstitch over stitching on the wrong side.

Mitring binding

Unfold one edge of binding and place against the raw fabric edge. Pin and stitch in place along first side up to the seam allowance at the turning point. Press up the binding over the stitched side at a 45 degree

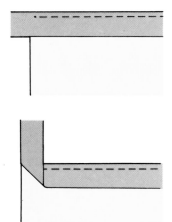

angle, then fold it back down on itself with the fold level with the first side. Stitch the next side beginning at the turning point. Trim and turn binding over the raw edge to the wrong side, folding the excess binding on both sides into mitres. Slipstitch remaining folded edge of binding over previous stitches on the wrong side. If the binding is wide, slipstitch across the mitre on the right side of the binding.

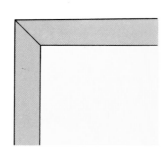

MEASURING FOR CURTAINS

Always follow the fixing instructions that come with your chosen track or pole, but if you are curtaining on an existing track measure from the top of the track or pole or wire to the desired length and add on the stated allowances for hems and top fixing.

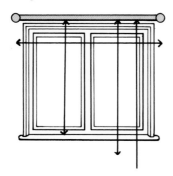

HAND STITCHES

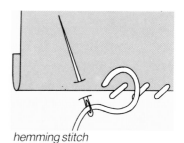

backstitch

hemming stitch

slipstitching

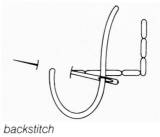

herringbone stitch

chain stitch

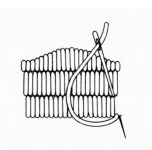

long and short stitch

satin stitch

encroaching satin stitch

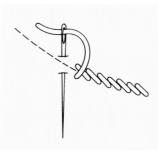

stem stitch

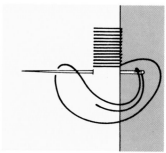

buttonhole stitch

SANDS, SEA AND SHORE

Minimal, single-colour designs, as wild and charming as the dunes and grasses of a lonely seashore, are worked on fabric chosen to echo the colours of northern seas. The loose cover and cushions were made by designer Janick Schoumacher to complement the lovely scenery from the windows of her holiday home. The idea of breaking down the clearcut line between inside and outside works very well, but the sofa could equally be used to set the scene for a room centred on a seascape picture.

Size: instructions show how to cut and fit the loose cover to your own sofa.

MATERIALS

Fabric – see below for quantity
12 skeins of DMC stranded
    cotton in white
Size 6 or 7 crewel needle
Large embroidery hoop
Zips for cushion covers – about
10cm (4in) shorter than
finished width of cushion
Six hooks and bars
Matching thread
Dressmakers' carbon paper

METHOD

THE CUSHION COVERS

▦ Measure one of your cushions and cut three pieces for cushion fronts to this size plus 1.5cm (⅝in) seam allowance all around.

▦ Trace the designs from the photographs and enlarge them as required (see page 14). Transfer to fabric, using dressmakers' carbon paper.

▦ Work with fabric stretched in an embroidery hoop, moving it as necessary. Using the photographs as stitch guides, embroider the grass in stem stitch, sand in French knots and water and dunes in satin stitch and encroaching satin stitch. Three strands of thread are used.

▦ When embroidery is complete, place each piece face downwards on a well padded surface and press it lightly, taking care not to crush the stitches.

▦ For each cushion back, cut a piece to the finished measurements plus 3cm (1¼in) on the width and 6cm (2½in) on the length. Cut in half across the width.

▦ Place back pieces with right sides together. Pin and tack together along the width, taking 1.5cm (⅝in) seam allowance. Stitch for 6.5cm (2⅝in) from each side. Press seam open. Place zip face down over seam, with teeth over tacked section. Pin, tack and then stitch from right side. Open zip.

▦ Matching outer edges, pin and stitch cushion front and back pieces together round outer edges, taking 1.5cm (⅝in) seam allowance. Trim and neaten seam allowance. Turn cover right side out, insert the cushion and close the zip.

THE LOOSE COVER

▦ To estimate fabric needed, it helps to draw chalk lines on a suitable floor space, the width of the fabric apart, and sketch in the shapes as you measure, bearing in mind matching stripes or patterns.

▦ Each part of the sofa is measured both ways, as shown in diagram, and measurements are written down. Except for front and arm panels, all pieces are cut out as rectangles, then trimmed and pin-fitted into place on sofa before stitching.

▦ On the fabric, mark out each rectangle, bearing in mind fabric design, then cut out each piece. Add 4cm (1½in) to any side which will form base hem, and 15cm (6in) tuck-in allowance to base of inside back and inside arms and to top and side edges of seat. Add 5cm (2in) to all other sides for fitting and seam allowances. Mark each piece with its name, and also the top and base.

▦ Mark centre of sofa back, inside back and seat with a row of pins. Fit outside back in place first; place fabric on sofa, matching centres, and pin in place.

▦ Repeat with inside back, putting tuck-in allowance at base. Pin to outside back around back and sides.

▦ Pin inside and outside arms in place in the same way, with tuck-in allowance on inside arms. Pin arms to inside back, clipping into fabric allowance if necessary to gain a good curve.

▦ Pin seat in place to inside back and arms, with tuck-in allowance at back. Taper tuck-in allowance from nothing at sofa front to full depth at back of seat. Pin tuck-in allowances together around seat.

▦ Place tracing paper to front arm panel and carefully mark outline. Use as template, adding seam and hem allowances as before. Cut a matching pair of front arm panels.

▦ Arrange excess fabric around one arm front into evenly-spaced darts, then make opposite arm exactly the same. Pin front panels in place, again making sure that the shaping of the panels will look identical when sewn.

▦ Check that cover fits well then mark all seamlines with chalk. Remove cover from sofa; tack and stitch pieces together in same order as pinned, leaving one back corner seam open for about two-thirds of its length for fastenings.

▦ For strength, stitch each seam again just inside previous stitching. Trim seam allowances to 1.2cm (½in) and neaten.

▦ Face the back opening: snip into seam allowance at the top of the opening point up to the stitching. Cut an 8cm (3¼in) wide

seascape sofa

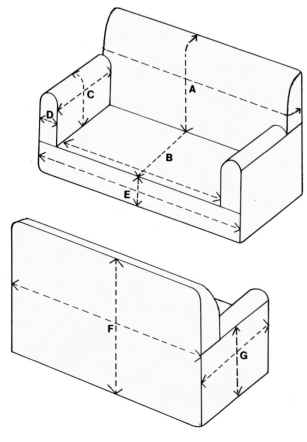

A *Inside back*

B *Seat*

C *Inside arm (×2)*

D *Front arm panel (×2)*

E *Front panel*

F *Back*

G *Outside arm (×2)*

Sofas differ widely in shape, and if yours has a thickly padded or clearly defined back, you may need an additional panel running up the sides and along the top of the back rest, joining the inside and outside back pieces. Similarly, if the arms extend beyond the seat section, the front arm panels must run from the top of the arms down to the floor, and the front panel will be correspondingly narrower.

strip of fabric twice the length of the opening. With opening held out straight, place strip with right side to wrong side of opening. Pin, tack and stitch, taking 1.5cm (⅝in) seam allowance. Turn in 1.5cm (⅝in) along remaining long edge of strip and bring over seam on right side of cover. Pin, tack and stitch in place. Fold facing to inside of cover. Stitch hooks and bars into faced opening, spacing them evenly.

▦ Replace cover over sofa and measure for the front panel, across complete sofa front. Remove cover. Cut out one piece to this size, adding 1.5cm (⅝in) for seams and 4cm (1½in) for base hem. Pin, tack and stitch in place to seat, front arm panel and to outside arm at each side. Trim and neaten seam allowances.

▦ Turn under a double 2cm (¾in) hem all round base edge of cover, so cover will just clear the floor. Pin, tack and stitch in place.

▦ Replace the cover over the sofa, pushing the tuck-in allowance down all round the seat. Add the cushions along the back.

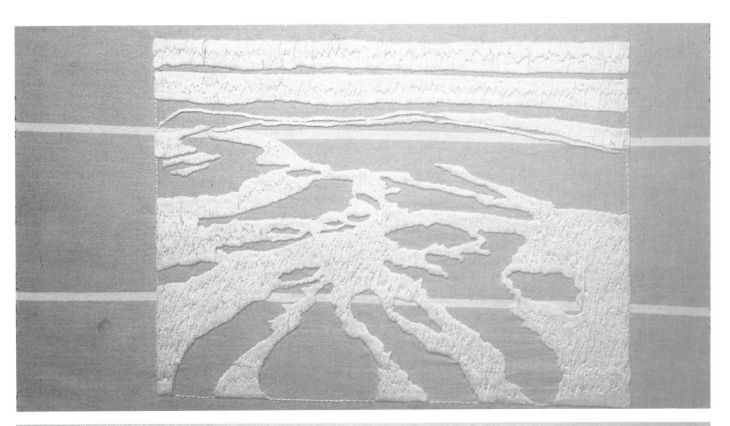

LITTLE WHITE TIES

A novel, even rather outrageous way of changing the entire appearance of your home, these white covers, like dust sheets, could be hiding virtually anything: is that an antique Louis XV table or is it laminated plastic – who can say? And are the real owners relaxing on the Orient Express while sophisticated intruders make use of their abandoned house? If you are bored with your surroundings, or the colours are too warm and suffocating for summer, or your old chairs need a facelift but don't merit the full treatment, here's one way to create an air of mystery and impermanence, and at the same time to turn everyday furnishings into white, sculptured objects.

Sizes: tablecloth 202cm×202cm (79½in×79½in); fireplace and chair covers to fit individual requirements.

MATERIALS

FOR THE TABLECLOTH
5m (5¾yd) of 115cm (45in) wide bleached calico
Matching thread
10m (11yd) of 13mm (½in) wide white binding tape

FOR THE FIREPLACE
Bleached calico – see below for quantity
Matching thread

FOR THE PLAIN CHAIR COVER
Bleached calico – see below for quantity
Matching thread

FOR THE BLACK AND WHITE COVERS
Bleached calico – see below for quantity
Black sewing cotton
or black fabric painting pen
Matching thread

METHOD

THE FIREPLACE COVER

▣ If you prefer, you could make this summer cover in a pastel or chintz fabric, but do not use it when the fire is lit, even if it seems to hang well clear of the flames. The cover is made from six pieces: one for the top (shelf) of the mantelpiece, two outer (side) pieces, one top front and two side fronts. Measure the length and depth of the top (shelf) of the mantelpiece, then measure from the sides of the shelf down to floor level. Cut out a piece for the top, adding 2cm (¾in) to the back (wall) edge and 1cm (⅜in) to all other edges. Cut two side pieces, adding 2cm (¾in) to the back (wall) edges, 4cm (1½in) to the base (floor) edges and 1cm (⅜in) to all other edges. For the front, measure from shelf to floor and from outer side to inner

(fireplace) side, for side pieces, and from inner side to side for front section. Cut side pieces, adding 4cm (1½in) to the base edges and 1cm (⅜in) to top and outer side edges. Cut out centre front, adding 4cm (1½in) to the base (floor) edge and 1cm (⅜in) to top edge.

▣ Pin, tack and stitch the outer sides to the top (shelf) piece, with right sides together and with plain seams, leaving 1cm (⅜in) unstitched at the front edges. Turn under a double 1cm (⅜in) hem along the entire back (wall) edge; pin, tack and stitch.

▣ For the fireplace front, cut 8cm (3¼in) wide strips of binding to run along both sides of front section and along inner (fireplace) side of each side section. Place each strip against the edge which is to be bound, with right sides together. Taking 2cm (¾in)

seam allowance, pin, tack and stitch together. Turn under 2cm (¾in) along remaining long edge of binding: bring binding over the raw edge and pin, tack and slipstitch to the back, over previous line of stitching. Bind remaining side edges.

▣ Lap bound edges of front over side sections: total width of

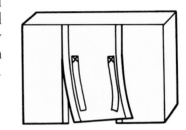

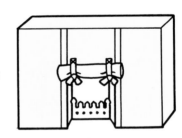

overlap 2cm (¾in) at each side. Pin, tack and stitch together down both sides of bound edge to the level of the top of the fireplace (inner edge).

▣ Cut out four strips, each 46cm×8cm (18in×3¼in), for tapes. Press in 1cm (⅜in) turnings all round, then fold each strip in half, with wrong sides together. Pin, tack and stitch all around each strip. Position two pairs of tapes on right and wrong side of centre piece about 3cm (1¼in) above top of fireplace opening and 15cm (6in) in from either side edge. Stitch tape ends in place.

▣ Place front to mantelpiece side (top) piece, matching top seams to corners of front section; pin, tack and stitch together.

▣ Turn up a double 2cm (¾in) wide base hem all around cover; pin, tack and stitch.

▣ Place over fireplace and check that it fits neatly. Roll up front and tie tapes together to hold.

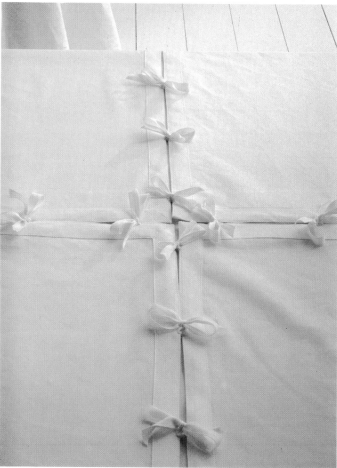

THE TABLECLOTH

▦ From fabric, cut out four 102cm (40¼in) squares. Also cut enough 4.2cm (1¾in) strips of binding to make up 16 lengths, one for each side of each fabric square. Cut 32 lengths of white binding tape, each 30cm (12in) long, for ties.

▦ Position ties on squares, four ties each on two joining edges of each square. Space the ties evenly, with short raw edge of tie matching the raw edge of the fabric, and the tie lying on the wrong side of the fabric. Make sure that all ties match on all four squares, so that the finished squares will join neatly.

▦ Taking a scant 6mm (¼in) seam allowance, stitch ties to fabric.

▦ With right side of binding to wrong side of fabric, and keeping ties lying flat on the fabric, pin, tack and stitch one strip of binding to one side of a fabric square, taking a 6mm (¼in) seam allowance. Begin and end stitching 6mm (¼in) in from each raw side edge. At each corner, fold back the binding at a 45 degree angle and press. Stitch remaining binding strips to edges in the same way.

▦ When all strips have been stitched in place, bring pressed corner lines together and stitch along the folds to make mitred corners. Trim corners, then turn under a 6mm (¼in) seam allowance all around border strips. Bring binding over to right side of fabric and topstitch in position, stitching close to both the inner and outer edges of the binding.

▦ Tie squares together to complete the cloth.

THE PLAIN CHAIR COVER

▦ Each chair is different, so your cover must to some extent be shaped to your particular chair, but there is no need for it to fit closely: the cover is supposed to be loose and just tied together at either side of the chair at the back. It is cut in five pieces: one piece runs from the base at the back, over the top of the chair and down across the seat and on to the base; two arm pieces run up from the base over each arm, meeting the main piece at the side, and two arm fronts join the arms to the main piece at the front of the chair.

▦ Measure the chair for the main piece, from front base to back base and taking the widest measurement to give the width (the piece must be cut wide enough to be brought round the front of the chair to join with the back at the sides). Cut out, adding 1.5cm (⅝in) for each side seam and 4cm (1½in) for each base hem. Cut out all other pieces in the same way.

▦ Lay the main piece on the chair, wrong side out. Bring the front over the sides at the back of the chair and pin at the top.

▦ Trim the back portion to meet the front and the side edges at

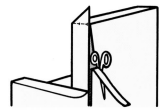

the back of the chair. Again with wrong sides out, pin the main arm sections to the main piece, trimming as necessary to get a good fit, but leaving 1.5cm (⅝in) seam allowances, and making sure that arm sections can easily be tied to back down side edges. Fit, pin and trim arm fronts to arms and main section. Mark all seamlines with pins or tailors' chalk, remembering that the fit should be generous rather than tight.

▦ Remove cover and stitch all seams. Finish off outside edges which meet down the back with binding, as for the fireplace cover. Make ties as for the fireplace cover and stitch them down the back edges in matching pairs. Turn up and stitch a double 2cm (¾in) hem at the base of the cover.

▦ Place cover over chair and tie bows across back edges.

THE BLACK AND WHITE COVERS

▦ The main piece runs from the top of the chair, down the front, across the seat and down to the floor level. Measure the back from top to floor level, and measure for two side pieces which run from the edge of the seat down to floor level and from the front edge to the back edge of the chair.

▦ Cut out all four pieces, adding 1.5cm (⅝in) seam allowances to all joining edges and 4cm (1½in) to the base edge.

▦ Join back to front, then join in the sides. Cut binding strips and bind the side edges at the back of the cover, as for fireplace. Make tapes as for fireplace and stitch in pairs along the bound edges.

▦ Place cover on chair, right side out, and gently mark in a design of your choosing, using a pencil. Remove the cover and work over the design lines, either with a close zigzag stitch or with a fabric painting pen. If you are using a

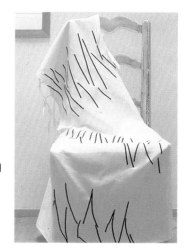

machine zigzag stitch, work from the centre of the design outwards, whenever possible, to ease out any puckers and avoid distorting the fabric. For the same reason, you may find that you get better results if you run over the lines twice, with a fairly open stitch.

LIGHT AS AIR

Fine white organdie, tucked into pleats or shaped into delicate border detailing makes the perfect complement to a glass table set with crystal and fine porcelain – guaranteed to make your soufflés, mousses and meringues a touch lighter! There are three different placemats to choose from: one is flanked by pleats at either side; one has a doubled border shaped into scallops and the third has a plain double-thickness border. The napkin has a simple border of pintucks running right around.

Size: each placemat measures approximately 48cm×36cm (19in×14¼in); napkin 25cm×25cm (10in×10in).

MATERIALS

70cm (¾yd) of 115cm (45in) wide organdie for any one placemat and napkin	*Paper – for scalloped edge mat only* *Matching thread*

METHOD

THE PLEATED MAT

▦ Cut a strip of organdie 82cm×38cm (33in×15¼in). Turn under a double 6mm (¼in) hem along both long edges; pin and tack. Zigzag stitch along both short edges.

▦ Fold fabric in half, bringing short edges together to find vertical centre of mat. Mark centre point at top and lower edges with pins. Measure out 12.5cm (5in) either way to find point A, stitching line of first pleat.

▦ With wrong sides together, fold fabric to make first pleat, 3.2cm (1⁵⁄₁₆in) deep, with the fold 15.7cm (6⁵⁄₁₆in) from the marked centre. Stitch the pleat with ordinary straight stitch. Refold the fabric to make the second pleat, 3cm (1¼in) deep, so that the stitching of the second fold will be just covered by the edge of the first pleat. Stitch, then turn back the last 5cm (2in) and stitch, to make the outer pleat. Make pleats on both sides in this way, with pleats facing outwards.

▦ To complete mat, topstitch along both top edges, holding pleats in position, and cover the stitching line of the inner pleat at either side with zigzag stitch or a machine embroidery stitch.

THE SCALLOPED EDGE MAT

▦ Take a piece of paper 48cm×36cm (19in×14¼in). Fold it in half and then in quarters. Using the base of a wine glass, mark scallops along the cut edges: one scallop should run round the corner and another scallop should run at either side from the first scallop up to the folded edge. Cut along the scallops and unfold the paper.

▦ Use this paper pattern to cut out two scalloped rectangles from fabric, adding a 6mm (¼in) seam allowance. On one piece, mark a rectangle measuring 34cm x 20cm (13¼in x 8in), centring it.

▦ Place the two pieces of fabric wrong sides together and stitch all around scalloped edge, taking 6mm (¼in) seam allowance. Cut out one side of the fabric only along the marked inner edge and turn the border right side out. Turn in a 6mm (¼in) single hem along the inner rectangular edge, clipping up to the corners if necessary to get a smooth edge. Stitch inner edge in position, either with straight topstitching or with a close zigzag stitch.

THE PLAIN BORDER MAT

▦ Make in the same way as the scalloped edge mat, but without shaping the edges. If desired, decorate the inner and outer edges with satin stitch or other machine embroidery stitching.

THE NAPKIN

▦ From fabric cut out a 30.5cm (12¼in) square. Pin and tack a double 6mm (¼in) hem all around napkin. Finish the edge with a row of machine embroidery or close zigzag stitch to hold and at the same time decorate the edge.

▦ Work a series of three 3mm (⅛in) deep pin tucks, spaced about 2.5cm (1in) apart, along each side of the napkin.

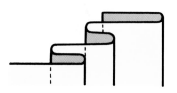

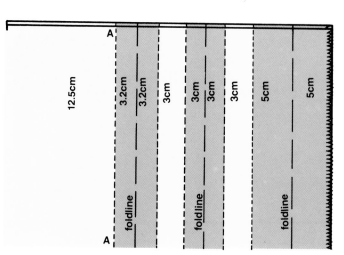

LACED BEDHEAD

The simplest ideas are often the most successful, like this elegantly sporty bedhead – a complete contrast to the more usual, highly padded variety, and much more in keeping with those who like their living spaces to be practical, uncluttered and stylish, but with a light touch of humour. The cover is so easy to make – just two rectangles of calico, one laced over the other – that you could sew it in an evening.

Size: the cover can be made to fit any rectangular bedhead.

MATERIALS

90cm (36in) wide calico – quantity will vary according to the height of the headboard: approximately 3m (3¼yd) for a 135cm (4ft 6in) wide bed and 2.2m (2½yd) for a 90cm (3ft) wide bed

White cord – approximately 4.5m (5yd) for a 135cm (4ft 6in) wide bed and 3m (3¼yd) for a 90cm

(3ft) wide bed
1.5m (1⅝yd) of 13mm (½in) wide white tape
6mm (¼in) diameter white eyelets and an eyelet punch
Matching thread
2.5cm (1in) thick foam, cut to the size of the headboard
All purpose adhesive

METHOD

▦ If you do not have a rectangular headboard, cut plywood to the desired size. Also check that the board can be fixed to the bed. Using adhesive, fix foam to the front of headboard.

▦ Measure the bedhead both ways. For the back, cut a rectangle of calico to this size, adding the bedhead thickness plus 19cm (7½in) to the height and twice the bedhead thickness plus 30cm (12in) to the width. For the front, cut a piece to the

bedhead measurement plus the thickness of the bedhead and 1cm (⅜in) on the height and less 6cm (2½in) on the width.

▦ Neaten the side and top edges of the front with zigzag stitch and turn these edges under for 5cm (2in). Pin and tack. Turn up the lower edge to make a double 2cm (¾in) hem; pin, tack and stitch.

▦ Turn under top and side edges of back piece for 5cm (2in) and press. Unfold. Turn under and stitch a double 2cm (¾in) hem at lower edge.

▦ Place back piece centrally over the back of the headboard, bringing sides and top over to the front (lower edge is level with lower edge of board). Pin to hold. Fold in top corner points, then turn in top and side edges to form mitred corners. Pin corners, then remove back from headboard and stitch mitred corners up to pressed lines 5cm (2in) from front edges.

▦ Turn under top and side edges along pressed lines and tack.

▦ Pin front and back together over headboard, with back overlapping front at top and side edges by 2cm (¾in). Mark positions for eyelets on top and side edges, 2.5cm (1in) from inner edges on back and 4.5cm (1¾in) from outer edges on front. Place eyelets about 10cm (4in) apart on each edge, and stagger the positions so that the cord will be threaded at an angle.

▦ Remove and unpin both sections and punch eyelets in place through folded thicknesses of fabric (this will hold hems in place). Also position two eyelets at either side of mitred corner.

▦ Cut tape into eight equal lengths and stitch to lower edges of cover at matching positions to make four pairs of ties.

▦ Replace front and back over headboard and, beginning at the base edge, lace the two pieces together, tucking the front section under the back for 2cm (¾in). At opposite edge, pull cord and knot behind last eyelet.

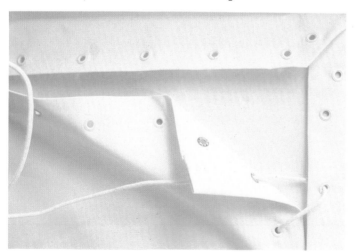

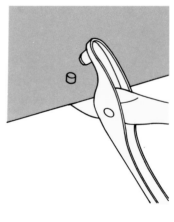

BEDROOM PAGEANTRY

There is more than a hint of medieval pomp and pageantry in this room, transformed from a straightforward bedroom into a royal tent by the simple addition of tabbed curtains, a luxuriously swathed and tied canopy and an unusual, envelope-like duvet cover with matching pillowcases. Great fun for anyone with a taste for the dramatic, this lavish and splendid effect is not in the least difficult to achieve.

Sizes: curtains and canopy to your required measurements; duvet cover 200cm×200cm (80in×80in); pillowcases 79cm×50cm (31½in×20in).

MATERIALS

CANOPY
Fabric – see below for quantity; the fabric should preferably have no very marked right and wrong sides
Matching thread
Two lengths of 1.5cm (⅝in) dowel, the width of the bed plus 20cm

(8in), and cords and hooks for hanging
Length of 5cm× 2cm (2in× ¾in) batten, the width of the bed
Screws to fix batten
Fabric adhesive or staples

FOR THE CURTAINS
Fabric – see below for quantity
Contrast fabric – small amount for curtain loops
5cm (2in) strip of iron-on interfacing the width of the curtain

3.5cm (1½in) diameter buttons – two for each tab required
Matching thread
Dowel pole for hanging
Brackets to fix dowel to window frame

FOR THE DUVET COVER AND PILLOWCASES
4.1m (4⅝yd) of 228cm (90in) wide sheeting
2.6m (3yd) of 228cm (90in) wide sheeting in a contrast pattern

Twenty-eight 3.5cm (1½in) diameter buttons
Matching thread

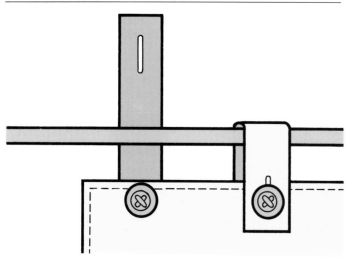

METHOD

THE CANOPY
▦ Fix hooks in ceiling and hang dowels about 220cm (88in) above floor level, one at the head and one at the foot of the bed. The batten will be screwed to the wall about 75cm (30in) above the bedhead.

▦ To measure for fabric, pin a length of string to the wall at batten height and take the string over the dowels and down to the floor, allowing for generous loops of fabric and sufficient at the foot of the bed to tie a loose knot and drape the remainder on the floor. For the width, allow one-and-half times the length of the batten.

▦ Cut out fabric, joining lengths if necessary to achieve the width with flat fell seams. Either leave selvedges or turn under a double 1cm (⅜in) hem down both long edges; pin, tack and stitch. Turn under a 1cm (⅜in) hem along base edge; pin, tack and stitch.

▦ Work two rows of gathering stitches along remaining short edge and pull up to fit batten, then fasten off.

▦ Paint the batten the same colour as the wall. When dry, fix the raw gathered edge of fabric to the 5cm (2in) side which will be against the wall. With fabric hanging down, fix batten to wall.

▦ Bring fabric up over both lengths of dowel; tie into a single knot and arrange in folds at floor level.

THE CURTAINS
▦ For each curtain required, fix dowel pole in position across window. Measure from dowel to chosen length and add 21cm (8¼in). Curtain width is one-and-a-quarter times the length of the dowel (this includes allowance for side hems).

▦ Cut out curtain and turn under a double 2cm (¾in) hem down both side edges. Pin in place, then turn under a double 5cm (2in) hem along base edge, mitring corners. Tack and stitch hems.

▦ Iron a 5cm (2in) strip of interfacing to wrong side of curtain at top, 1cm (⅜in) down

from raw edge of fabric. Fold and press fabric over top edge of interfacing, then bring folded edge over to form a double 5cm (2in) hem. Pin, tack and topstitch in place.

▦ Loops are spaced evenly at intervals of about 15cm (6in) apart. For each loop cut two pieces of contrast fabric measuring 8cm×23cm (3¼in×9¼in). With right sides together, pin, tack and stitch around the edges, leaving a small opening. Trim and turn to right side. Turn in opening edges and slipstitch to close.

▦ Work vertical buttonholes at either end of each loop, centring them, and positioning them to start 2.5cm (1in) up from ends. At each loop position on curtain, stitch a button to either side of the hemmed edge, 2.5cm (1in) from top and bottom edges of hem.

▦ To hang, button each loop to the back of the curtain, take it over the dowel and then button it to the front.

THE DUVET COVER AND PILLOWCASES

▦ Cut fabrics as follows: for duvet front cut one piece 203cm×205.5cm (81¼in × 82¼in) from the larger fabric, and one piece 203cm × 146.5cm (81¼in × 57½in) for flap, from same fabric but with pattern running crosswise. For duvet back, cut one piece 203cm (81¼in) square from second main fabric. For each pillowcase, cut two pieces, one from main fabric and one from contrast, each 78cm×53cm (31¼in × 21¼in).

▦ Fold flap section in half widthways so that folded piece measures 146.5cm×101.5cm (57½in×40⅝in). Mark a point 56.5cm (22⅝in) down raw side edges and draw a line from here up to the folded centre. Cut along this line through both layers of fabric, then unfold fabric.

▦ Cut and join 11cm (4¾in) wide strips of contrast fabric to make a piece long enough to bind the

pointed edge. Fold in 1.5cm (⅝in) along both long edges and press well. Unfold.

▦ Place strip to right side of flap with pressed seamline 4cm (1½in) from raw edge of flap. Pin, tack and stitch, taking 1.5cm (⅝in) seam allowance. Turning in other pressed edge of binding, bring binding over flap edge to cover previous seamline. Topstitch in place.

▦ Work 16 buttonholes, eight on either side of pointed centre, at evenly spaced intervals along the band.

▦ Turn over and sew a double 2cm (¾in) hem along top edge of main front piece. Place flap on front cover, with raw edge projecting 1.5cm (⅝in) beyond

hemmed edge. Mark positions of buttons on front cover and stitch in place. Fasten buttons through buttonholes.

▦ Tack front pieces together at overlapping sides. Place front on back, right sides together. Pin, tack and stitch all around, taking care to leave hemmed edge at top of main front piece free. Stitch again 3mm (⅛in) beyond first row of stitching. Trim and neaten seam allowances together. Turn completed cover right side out.

▦ Take pillowcase pieces and bind one raw short edge of each piece with an 11cm (4¾in) wide strip of contrast fabric, following the same method as for duvet.

▦ For each pillowcase, take two contrasting pieces and join them together along the two long edges and unbound short edge, using French seams (see page 14). Mark and work six evenly spaced buttonholes along one bound edge then stitch buttons to inside of opposite bound edge.

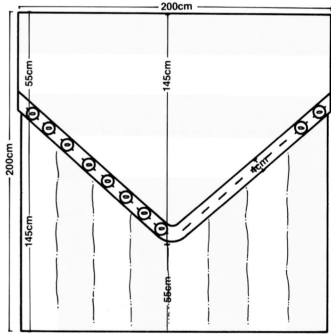

The measurements given show the dimensions of the completed cover. The binding must be eased round the point of the flap, turning it into a curve rather than a point. If you find it difficult to do this neatly, you may find it easier to make a mitred fold in the binding.

PRISMATIC NET

Let the sun filter into your room through a fine net curtain decorated with bright triangles set at random, sending patches of multi-coloured light dancing over your walls and floor. This unusual and amusing idea is very quick to make, but it gives you plenty of scope to indulge your creative side.

Size: to fit your window.

MATERIALS

White or light-coloured net fabric
   (see below for quantity)
Oddments of net fabric in a range
   of colours

Eyelets and eyelet punch
Matching thread
2cm (¾in) diameter curtain pole
   plus fixing brackets

METHOD

▥ Measure the window and cut out one piece of net fabric to this length plus 28cm (11in) for hem and casing and to one-and-a-half times the finished width. If necessary to gain the curtain width, cut out two or more lengths and stitch together with flat fell seams to achieve the correct size. Remember when calculating the width to measure across the full desired width, not just the inside width of the window frame.

▥ Turn under a double 2cm (¾in) hem on both side edges and pin. Turn under a double 5cm (2in) hem along base edge and pin. Mitre the bottom corners. Tack and stitch all around the hems.

▥ At the top, turn under a double 9cm (3½in) hem/casing. Pin, tack and stitch across, close to the folded lower edge. Stitch across hem/casing again, just below top edge.

▥ Make a card template of an equilateral triangle with 10cm (4in) sides. Using template and coloured pencils, mark triangles on net oddments and cut out.

▥ Lay the curtain right side up on the floor or other large flat surface. Selecting points at random, pin two or three triangles at a time to the curtain, moving triangles so that they do not lie directly on top of each other. Fix each group with an eyelet.

▥ Hang the curtain on the pole.

SUNNY DAYS

Enhance the joys of summer – the long hot days, the long cool drinks and the lazy chatter of friends – with a charming and elegant deckchair and matching parasol. Choose the prettiest chintz you can find for the chair cover, then copy one of the motifs onto a plain parasol: the idea is so simple, yet so perfect a way to set a summer scene. If you are not sure whether your upholstery fabric is quite strong enough for a deckchair, back it according to the instructions given below.

MATERIALS

FOR THE DECKCHAIR COVER

Printed cotton fabric – see below for quantity
Plain white cotton fabric (as above)
Iron-on interfacing

Matching thread
Upholstery nails or heavy-duty staples
Deckchair

FOR THE PARASOL

Tracing paper
Dressmakers' carbon paper
Oiled stencil board
Craft knife
Fabric paints

Adhesive tape
Stencil brush or small piece of sponge
Large plain white umbrella or parasol

METHOD

THE DECKCHAIR COVER

▦ Lay the deckchair flat and measure across the top or bottom fixing bar. Add 12cm (5in) to this to find the width. Cut printed fabric to this width and sufficiently long to wrap around the fixing bars and fasten. Cut white cotton to the same size.

▦ Match the two fabrics with wrong sides together; pin and tack together all around the outer edge. Make up the cover treating the two fabrics as one piece.

▦ Cut a 3cm (1¼in) wide strip of iron-on interfacing the length of each side of cover. Lay on wrong side against the outer edge at either side of the cover and iron in place. Turn over a double 3cm (1¼in) wide hem along each side edge. Pin, tack and stitch both hems in place, stitching close to both edges for strength.

▦ Turn under both short ends and fasten to the deckchair frame with upholstery nails or heavy-duty staples.

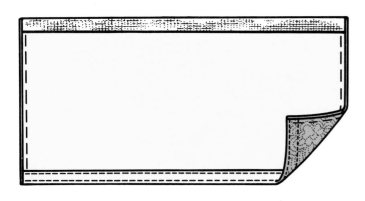

THE PARASOL

▦ Trace off a motif from the printed fabric, simplifying the design if necessary for the stencil outline. Stems and fine details of shading can be painted in freehand afterwards.

▦ If you have never tried stencilling before, keep to a relatively simple, clearly defined outline. A single, large-scale motif would in any case be more effective on a large parasol than an intricately detailed pattern. If you are not sure how the completed motif will look, make a sample painting on fabric before cutting the stencil. To do this, use your final tracing (see bottom left picture) and dressmaker's carbon paper to copy the outline onto a spare piece of fabric, then colour it in with fabric paints.

▦ Place the finished stencil against the open parasol and hold it with adhesive tape. Using a small piece of sponge or a stencil brush, dab the paint over the stencil.

▦ When the paint has dried, remove the stencil and mark the next section. Fill in any extra details such as leaf veins, by hand, using a fine brush.

▦ If necessary (see manufacturer's instructions) fix the paint to the fabric with a hot iron.

▦ For a finishing touch, make yourself a straw hat to match: take an ordinary straw hat with a wide brim; cut out a motif from the fabric, leaving a margin of 6mm (¼in) all around. Turn under and tack the seam allowance, then slipstitch the motif to the hat. Alternatively, use bonding fabric and simply iron on the motif.

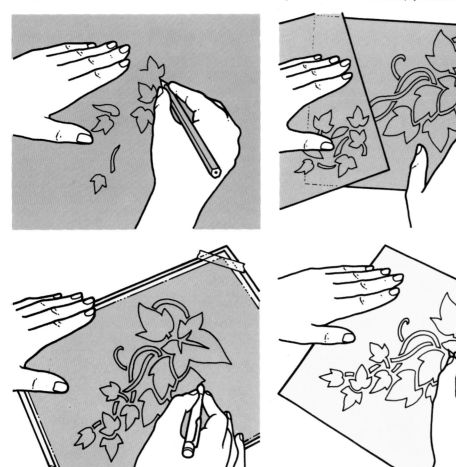

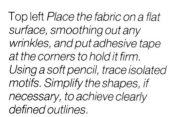

Top left *Place the fabric on a flat surface, smoothing out any wrinkles, and put adhesive tape at the corners to hold it firm. Using a soft pencil, trace isolated motifs. Simplify the shapes, if necessary, to achieve clearly defined outlines.*

Top right *Once you have traced all the motifs, cut them out from tracing paper so that you can move the pieces around to create a pleasing arrangement.*
Bottom left *Trace over the arrangement, then place carbon paper between the tracing and* the board. Tape the tracing in position and go over the lines with a ball-point pen.
Bottom right *Make any final improvements to the stencil with a pencil, then cut out the shapes with a craft knife.*

PROVENCAL PICNIC SET

As soon as warm weather approaches, you can prepare to expand your lifestyle to include elegant outdoor meals and picnics, adding a touch of sophistication with this pretty bordered tablecloth and matching picnic bag. They are very easy to make: the cloth just has a simple border in a contrast fabric; the bag is padded and then lined with a contrast fabric, the patchwork effect coming from the handles which run down the bag to meet at the base. The skill lies in choosing a subtle contrast of fabrics suited to good food and an easy life under the shade of the trees.

Sizes: tablecloth 141cm x 141cm (55½in x 55½in); bag approximately 45cm x 52cm (17½in x 20½in).

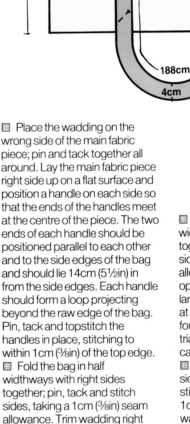
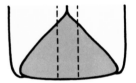

MATERIALS

FOR THE TABLECLOTH
1.3m (1½yd) of 128cm (50in) wide printed cotton fabric
1.5m (1¾yd) of 128cm (50in) wide printed cotton fabric in a contrast design
Matching thread

FOR THE BAG
60cm (¾yd) of 128cm (50in) wide printed cotton fabric
1m (1yd) of 128cm (50in) wide printed cotton fabric in a contrast design
1m (1yd) of 90cm (36in) wide lightweight wadding
Matching thread

METHOD

THE TABLECLOTH
▦ From the main fabric cut one piece 122cm (48in) square. For the border, cut four contrast pieces each 144cm×23cm (56¾in×9in).
▦ Fold each border strip in half lengthwise. At the corners, bring the short raw edges up to meet along the folded edge and press. Cut along the pressed lines (see page 15).
▦ Stitching in line with the mitred points, and with right sides together, join the strips into a circle, taking 1.5cm (⅝in) seams and stopping 1cm (⅜in) short of long sides of strips. Trim and refold strips right sides out.
▦ Turn in edges of border for 1cm (⅜in) on both sides of strip and press. Place border round central square, so that edges of border overlap those of the square for 1cm (⅜in). Pin, tack and topstitch.
▦ Work a close zigzag stitch all around the tablecloth, covering the border join.

THE BAG
▦ From main fabric cut out one piece 96cm×58cm (37¾in× 22¾in) for bag. Repeat to cut out one piece the same size from wadding and one from contrast.
▦ For handles, from contrast fabric cut four lengths each 95cm x 10cm (37½in x 4in). Place short ends of two handle pieces with right sides together; pin, tack and stitch, taking 1cm (⅜in) seam allowance to form a handle 188cm x 10cm (70¼in x 4in). Repeat for second handle. Press seams open.
▦ Fold one handle in half lengthwise with right sides together. Pin, tack and stitch long edge taking 1cm (⅜in) seam allowance and leaving an opening centrally in one side. Trim and turn to right side. Turn in opening edges in line with the remainder of the seam and slipstitch together to close. Press, then zigzag stitch raw ends to close and neaten. Repeat, to make up the second handle in the same way.

▦ Place the wadding on the wrong side of the main fabric piece; pin and tack together all around. Lay the main fabric piece right side up on a flat surface and position a handle on each side so that the ends of the handles meet at the centre of the piece. The two ends of each handle should be positioned parallel to each other and to the side edges of the bag and should lie 14cm (5½in) in from the side edges. Each handle should form a loop projecting beyond the raw edge of the bag. Pin, tack and topstitch the handles in place, stitching to within 1cm (⅜in) of the top edge.
▦ Fold the bag in half widthways with right sides together; pin, tack and stitch sides, taking a 1cm (⅜in) seam allowance. Trim wadding right back to seamline and turn bag right side out. Turn up base points of bag to side seam, forming a 4cm (1½in) triangle. Pin and tack, then topstitch down both sides of each side seam, catching in triangle at base.

▦ Fold bag lining in half widthways with right sides together; pin, tack and stitch sides, taking 1cm (⅜in) seam allowance and leaving an opening centrally in one side large enough to turn bag through at a later stage. Fold up ends as for outer cover, but forming the triangles on the wrong side and catch-stitching them in place.
▦ Place lining over bag with right sides together. Pin, tack and stitch all around top edge, taking 1cm (⅜in) seam allowance. Trim wadding right back to seamline and turn bag to right side. Turn in opening edges of lining in line with the remainder of the seam and slipstitch to close. Push lining down inside bag and, if necessary, catch to main fabric and wadding at base corners.

LAZY DAYS

There are few better ways of unwinding and relaxing than to swing lazily to and fro in a hammock on a warm summer's day, and this particular version, with its bright creole colours and attractive plaited ties, makes a lovely garden ornament even when it is not in use. Choose a good, strong fabric and check before buying that the weft threads can easily be removed. Pulling out the threads can be a time consuming business but it is very simple and there is no reason why all the potential users of the hammock, children included, should not join in its making.

Size: approximately 160cm × 150cm (64in × 60in), excluding plaits.

MATERIALS

4m (4½yd) of 150cm (60in) wide woven cotton fabric	Cotton yarn in a toning colour
1300mm (52in) length of 40mm (1½in) diameter dowel	Two painted wood napkin rings, purchased to fit after plaiting is complete
1.4m (1½yd) of 2.5cm (1in) wide webbing	15mm (¾in) tacks
Tacks	Matching thread

METHOD

▦ Mark the centre of the fabric, then mark 80cm (32in) on either side of the centre. Work two rows of zigzag stitching across the fabric width at these points.

▦ Unravel all the weft threads from both ends of the fabric, beyond the lines of the zigzag stitching.

▦ Divide the loose strands into bunches of about sixty strands and temporarily hold – make sure that the bunches look the same.

▦ Working with a bunch at a time, divide the bunch into three even sections and work together in a conventional three-strand plait to the end of the strands. Temporarily hold the end with an elastic band. Cut an 80cm (32in) length of yarn and hold the end against the end of the plait, bind the remaining yarn round the end of the plait, covering the yarn end as well as the strand ends.

Thread the end of the yarn back through the binding.

▦ Turn under the selvedge for 1cm (⅜in) on each side of the centre section; pin, tack and stitch in place.

▦ Cut one length of dowel 1000mm (40in) long and two pieces each 150mm (6in) long. Drill a 25mm (1in) hole centrally in each 150mm (6in) piece. Measure the distance across the short piece and mark this length on each end of longer piece. Shave down both ends up to the marks so they will fit snugly into the holes. Gently hammer in place.

▦ Gather all the plaits together at one side and push through a napkin ring. Thread one end of webbing through the ring. Wind the webbing over the dowel end and hammer tacks firmly in place to hold. Knot plaits round T-shaped end, to hold securely. Repeat at opposite side of bar.

HORSE BAG

This witty laundry bag, made in sturdy wipe-clean fabric, is designed to amuse but also serves the practical purpose of keeping your child's dirty clothes tidily hidden away. And proud owners of a real horse can use the bag to carry the grooming kit or muddy riding boots.

MATERIALS

1m (1yd) of 140cm (54in) wide plasticized fabric
3m (3¼yd) of yellow covered piping cord
60cm (¾yd) of white fringed braid

Suitable filling
2.3m (2½yd) of thick white cord
Eyelets
Black and white fabric paint
Dressmakers' pattern paper
Matching threads

METHOD

⊞ Draw up the patterns for the head, ear and gusset from diagrams, and cut out as stated. For the bag cut one piece 99cm × 58.5cm (39in × 23in) and a 33cm (13in) diameter circle for the bag base.

⊞ Make up the ears: working right side up, position covered piping cord along two sides of two ear pieces; tack in place. Place the ears right sides together in pairs with remaining plain ears; stitch sides, catching in piping. Trim and turn to right side. Fill each ear and stitch across base. Fold the ears in half matching Fs; stitch from D to E.

⊞ Working right side up, position covered piping round front of each head piece from A to C. Place one long edge of gusset to each head piece in turn; pin and stitch in place, leaving opening between As. Trim and turn to right side. Fill head and close opening. Stitch ears to top of head, matching points E to A.

⊞ Position a length of fringed braid along one short edge – the back – of bag piece, starting 1.5cm (⅝in) above the bottom edge and finishing 5cm (2in) below the top. Fold bag piece in

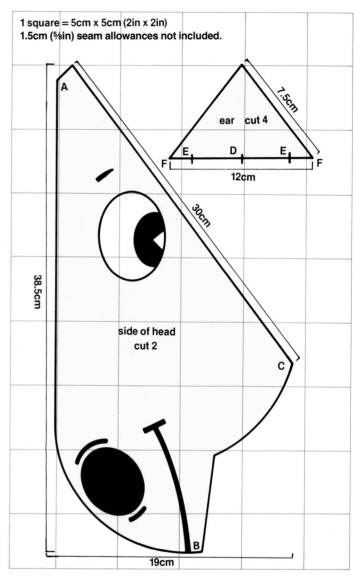

1 square = 5cm x 5cm (2in x 2in)
1.5cm (⅝in) seam allowances not included.

ear cut 4
7.5cm
12cm
E D E
F F
30cm
38.5cm
side of head cut 2
A
C
B
19cm

half right sides together, matching raw edges; pin and stitch back seam, catching in braid.

⊞ Staystitch round bag base, 1.5cm (⅝in) from outer edges. Working right side up, position piping cord round base. Cut a slightly longer length than needed and, at the join, unpick the bias covering and sew the ends together to make a continuous strip; unravel the cord ends and trim strands to different lengths, then twist them together to make a neat join. Fold covering back over cord.

⊞ Snip into allowance up to stitching all round base. Pin and

stitch bag base to base edge of bag piece. Turn down 5cm (2in) along top edge of bag; pin and stitch. Turn bag to right side.

⊞ Place horse head on bag at opposite side to back seam, 3cm (1¼in) from bag top; stitch in place by hand. Fold the remaining length of fringing into three and stitch to top of head.

⊞ Fix eight eyelets into the top edge of the bag, spacing them about 12cm (4¾in) apart. Fix two eyelets to base of bag, either side of back seam. Thread cord through the eyelets and fasten together with a knot.

⊞ Following diagram, paint in the eyes and nostrils.

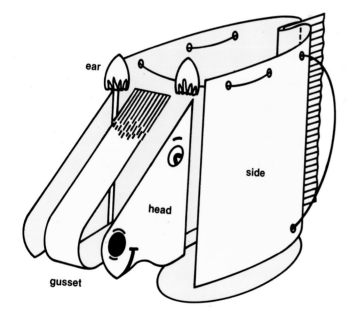

ear
side
head
gusset

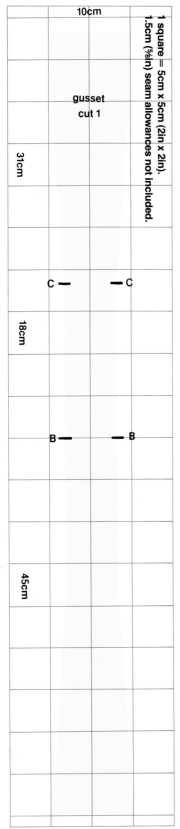

10cm

gusset
cut 1

31cm

C — — C

18cm

B — — B

45cm

1 square = 5cm x 5cm (2in x 2in).
1.5cm (⅝in) seam allowances not included.

PRECIOUS PURSES

These little purses, stitched in old-fashioned petit point, have an antique charm and are perfect for keeping your rings, bracelets and necklaces safely to hand. They would look delightful displayed in your bedroom rather than being hidden away in a drawer.

MATERIALS FOR SMALL PURSE

2 pieces of double-thread 18-gauge canvas, each 17cm (7in) × 13cm (5in)
2 pieces of dark green lining

fabric, each 11cm (4¼in) × 8cm (3in)
Matching sewing thread
Tapestry needle size 24

Threads
Anchor stranded cotton
2 skeins of **dark green** 212
1 skein of each of the following colours: **pink** 72, 75, 77; **green** 230, 240, 257; **mauve** 110; **red** 10, 46, 334

Embroidery Stitches
Tent stitch, back stitch, herringbone stitch.

METHOD FOR SMALL PURSE

Working the front and back pieces:
▥ Run a vertical and a horizontal line of tacking thread through the centres of each piece of canvas, to help with the positioning of the floral design. Match these lines to the corresponding squares of the chart to find the centre of the design.
▥ Working from the centre outwards, embroider the design from the chart in tent stitch, following the picture carefully.
▥ When the embroidery is completed, block it (see page 45), making sure that the front and the back pieces are exactly the same size.
▥ To make up the purse, trim away the surplus canvas round each piece of embroidery, leaving a margin of 1cm (⅜in).
▥ Using back stitch, join the front and back pieces.
▥ Turn over the 1cm (⅜in) margin at the top of the bag and secure it neatly with a row of herringbone stitch.
▥ Cut out the lining 1cm (⅜in) larger than the completed embroidery and join the seam. Turn and press a 1cm (⅜in) hem round the top of the lining and slipstitch it to the top of the bag,

leaving a 2cm (¾in) gap at one side over the seam.
▥ Make a twisted cord approximately 16cm (6in) long from 8 lengths of stranded cotton in dark green and decorate it with a tassel as shown in the photograph.
▥ Slipstitch the cord to the top of the bag, tucking the two ends into the gap in the lining. Stitch across the gap to secure the ends of the cord.

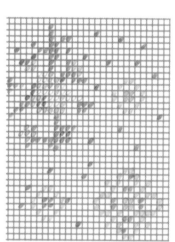

Pattern for small purse.

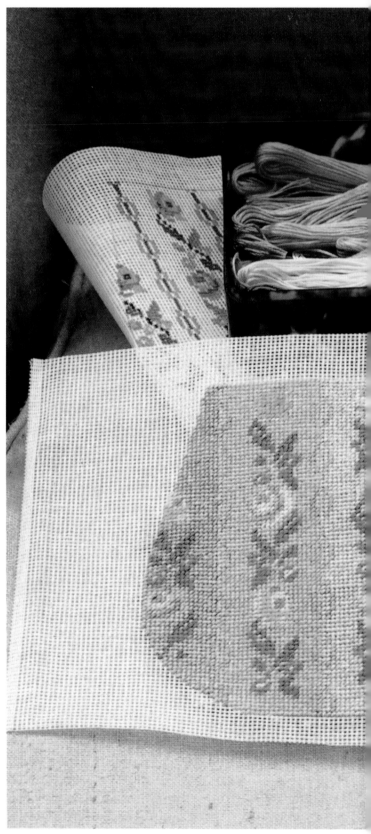

MATERIALS FOR LARGE PURSE

2 pieces of double-thread 18-gauge canvas, each 22cm (9in) × 18cm (7in)
40cm (16in) × 8cm (3in) double-thread 18-gauge canvas
2 pieces of pale grey fabric, each 17cm (7in) × 13cm (5in)
1 piece of the same fabric measuring 35cm (14in) × 5cm (2in)
Matching sewing thread
Tapestry needle size 24

Threads

Anchor stranded cotton
2 skeins of each of the following colours:
pale grey 398; **peach** 8; **pale green** 203; **beige** 852
1 skein of each of the following colours:
green 214, 227, 258; **blue** 118; **dark peach** 9; **pink** 778, 868; **ecru**

Embroidery Stitches

Tent stitch, herringbone stitch, back stitch.

METHOD FOR LARGE PURSE

▦ Run a vertical and a horizontal line of tacking thread through the centres of each piece of canvas to help with the positioning of the floral design. Match these lines to the corresponding squares of the chart to find the centre of the design.

▦ Working from the centre outwards embroider the design in tent stitch following the picture carefully.

▦ To make the gusset: work a strip of tent stitch nine stitches wide and approximately 33cm (13in) long, using the pale grey thread. When the embroidery is completed, block it carefully (see opposite), making sure that the front and back pieces are exactly the same size.

▦ Trim away the surplus canvas round each piece of embroidery leaving a margin of 1cm (⅜in).

▦ Using back stitch and the pale grey thread, join one edge of the gusset to the front piece and then the other edge of the gusset to the back piece.

▦ Turn over the 1cm (⅜in) margin round the top of the bag and secure with a row of herringbone stitch.

▦ Cut out the lining 1cm (⅜in) larger than the finished embroidered front, back and gusset and join the seams. Turn and press a 1cm (⅜in) hem round the top of the lining.

▦ Make a twisted cord approximately 1m (1yd) long from 10 lengths of stranded cotton. Decorate it with a tassel as shown in the photograph and sew each end of the cord securely to the inside of the gusset on the bag.

▦ Slipstitch the lining in place.

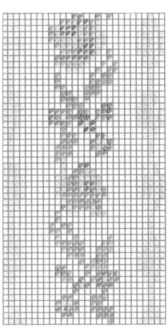

Pattern for large purse.

CANVASWORK TECHNIQUES

Canvaswork is a beautiful form of needlework that is usually worked on special embroidery canvas which is made of evenly woven cotton or linen. However, any fabric with evenly spaced holes can be used for canvaswork. It produces a firm, hard-wearing finish which is suitable for many decorative purposes around the home such as cushions, chair covers and rugs.

Types of canvas
There are two main types of canvas – single (mono) or double. Single canvas consists of a grid of horizontal and vertical threads. Double canvas has two strands for every thread so making it more adaptable because you can stitch between the small spaces as well as in the large holes. The size or gauge of the canvas is measured by a mesh count which denotes the number of holes (or sometimes threads when talking about mono canvas) to the centimetre or inch. For example, 18-gauge canvas has 72 holes to 10cm or 18 holes to the inch.

Double canvas is more versatile. You can work small stitches – or petit point – by using the spaces between the pairs of threads. This produces fine, detailed needlework.

Canvas is available in white or antique for use with light or dark colours.

Threads
A wide range of threads can be used for canvaswork. The important point is that the thread fills the holes. For a large gauge canvas, you would not want to use a stranded cotton, for example.

There are many materials to choose from, though wool and cotton are the most popular. Always buy the amount of yarn specified in the list of materials. Tensions in canvaswork vary a lot and the yarn used depends on the stitch too. You may have difficulty finding the correct dye lot again if you run out of yarn.

Preparing the canvas
Cut the piece of canvas to size, leaving at least 8cm (3in) all around the area to be stitched. To prevent it fraying, either place masking tape over the raw edges on all sides, sew on a length of bias binding or turn over the edge and hem.

When working canvaswork, the design can be copied square by square from a chart. You need to find the centre and work outwards from this point. If the centre is not marked on your chart, find it by counting the squares and mark it clearly.

Now take the prepared canvas and sew a line of tacking stitches from the top to the bottom and from one side of the canvas to the other. They should intersect at the middle, and you can use this to correspond with the centre point on the chart.

Getting started
Working with a thread about 50cm (20in) long, make a knot in the end or leave a tail and go in from the front a little way from the area you are going to work. This knot or tail of thread can then be worked over and cut off later.

Tent stitch
This is the most commonly used stitch in canvaswork. It is worked in horizontal rows backwards and forwards across the canvas, creating small even stitches on the front and even longer stitches at the back. This is a good padded stitch making it ideal for seats. When worked on small-gauge canvas, it is also known as petit point.

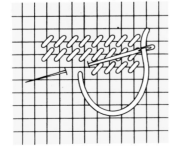

Bring the needle up through a hole and insert it again in the previous hole on the row above. Bring the needle out again on the lower row, one hole further along.

Half cross stitch
This stitch looks the same as tent stitch from the front of the canvas but at the back it forms straight stitches and takes up less thread. It is not as hard-wearing as tent stitch.

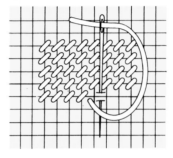

Work from left to right, bringing the needle up in the lower row and inserting it one hole along in the row above. Bring the needle back out again directly beneath the one you just entered. To work another row, turn the work upside down.

Blocking the canvas
A completed piece of canvaswork must be blocked to straighten the grain of the canvas, which becomes distorted after stitching, even if you have used an embroidery frame.

For blocking, you will need a piece of wood or blockboard slightly larger than the piece of embroidery, a clean sheet of polythene or paper, rustproof tacks, a hammer, a tape measure or steel rule and a sponge or water spray.

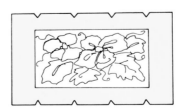

If the canvas has a selvedge, cut small nicks along these edges to ensure that it stretches evenly. Damp the piece of canvaswork all over with the spray or a wet sponge. Place the embroidery face down on the board which you have previously covered with polythene or paper in order to protect the stitching.

Lightly hammer the tacks in the middle of the top and bottom of the surplus canvas, stretching it gently downwards. Repeat for the sides, checking that the warp and weft threads of the canvas are at right angles to each other.

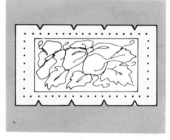

Working outwards from the centre of each side, insert more tacks at 2cm (¾in) intervals, stretching the canvas gently as you go. When all four sides are secured to the board, check the size and shape of the canvas to make sure that the stretching is even and adjust the tacks where necessary. When you are sure the canvaswork is the correct shape, hammer all the tacks in securely.

Spray or sponge the canvas again so that it is evenly damp and leave it to dry at room temperature for several days. Remove tacks and complete the project, trimming any excess canvas around the edges of the canvaswork as necessary.

Pressing canvas
To press canvaswork, remove it from the frame, sew in and cut off any loose threads and take out any tacking stitches. Place the work face down on a towel or cloth and press lightly with an iron and a damp cloth.

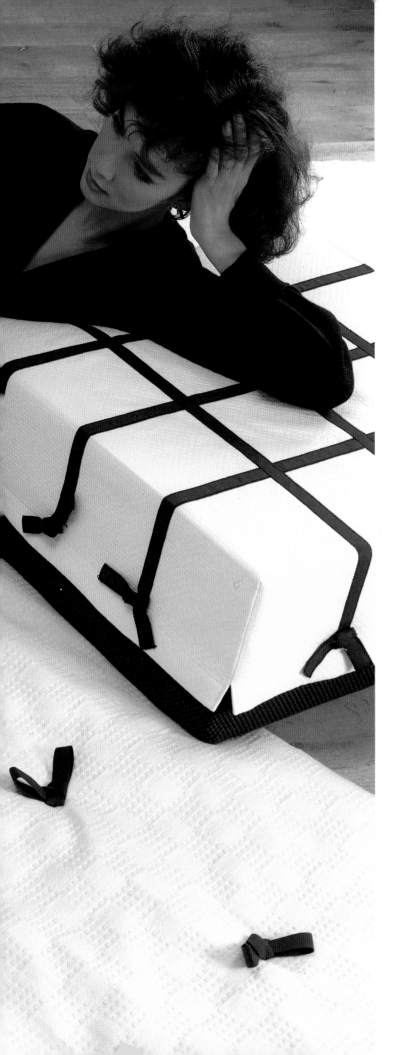

APPLIQUÉ

BASIC ESSENTIALS

Appliqué is one of the simplest and most adaptable ways of decorating cloth. The technique can be used to create fabric pictures, imitation patchwork effects and finishing touches on bed and table linen. It is also an ingeniously decorative method of repair.

Appliqué is often combined with other techniques such as patchwork, quilting and machine embroidery. The simplest form – known as appliqué perse – uses motifs cut from the pattern on a fabric and then applied directly to the background fabric. Traditional appliqué uses different fabrics, colours and embroidery stitching to build up the motif in layers.

Huge fruits and fan and cup shapes have been used to decorate this tablecloth which is even more eye-catching with the combination of patterned and plain fabrics.

Choosing fabrics

A wide range of fabrics can be used for appliqué, but some are easier to sew than others or are preferable because they are easier to clean. Although you can use old clothes and jumble sale finds, be sure that the fabric is still in good condition and has plenty of wear left in it. Non-fraying fabrics such as felt and net are ideal for beginners.

Because appliqué fabrics are sewn to a background, you can mix different weights and types of fabric in the same work, but for beginners, the easiest fabric to use is pure dress-weight cotton. Man-made fibres or polyester/cotton mixtures can be used but they tend to be springy, which makes them more difficult to shape and sew.

For the background, choose a firm fabric such as a good-quality cotton, which will wear well. Do not, however, choose one that is so firm that it creates sewing problems.

Making templates

You will need a template for each separate piece to be applied. Start by making a full-scale drawing of the design, then make a tracing of this, numbering each individual piece.

Take a second sheet of tracing paper and make a tracing of each numbered piece and then cut these tracings out. You can either use them as templates or stick them to thin card, which will give you a firmer edge.

Marking and cutting

Place the template right side up on the right side of the chosen fabric. Mark round the edge with a well-sharpened pencil in a colour close to that of the fabric. The applied pieces will be easier to sew and will blend in with the background more smoothly if you try to cut them so that the grainlines of the pieces lie in the same direction as the grainlines of the background fabric, so use your design drawing as a reference when marking.

Pieces that are machine sewn should be cut out without seam allowances. For hand-sewn pieces, leave a 6mm (¼in) seam allowance all round when cutting out. Very faintly pencil the number of the piece on the back of the patch.

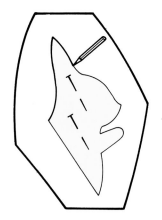

Preparing and positioning

Machine-sewn pieces are pinned and tacked directly to the fabric. Hand-sewn pieces must first be prepared by turning under and tacking the seam allowances (if one piece overlaps another, the portion which will lie underneath need not be turned and tacked).

It may help you to achieve a good line if you first staystitch round the piece, stitching within the seam allowance and close to the inner line, either by machine or by hand, using a small running stitch.

On convex curves, as on a sun shape, it is a good idea to run a gathering thread round the curve. Take small stitches, keeping within the seam allowance, but starting with a knot on the right side of the fabric so that the thread can easily be removed. Take notches out of the seam allowance at regular intervals to remove excess fullness.

On concave curves, clip halfway to the seamline at regular intervals, using sharp embroidery scissors.

Cut across tops of points, within seam allowance, and turn them under; turn down cut point first, then fold in the sides.

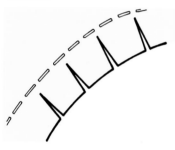

Tack with small tacking stitches, pressing the edge firmly with your fingers as you tack.

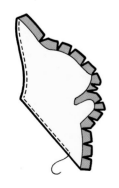

When all the pieces are prepared, position them on the fabric, using your design tracing as a guide. Pin and then tack the pieces, stitching about 4mm (⅙in) from the edge.

Hand sewing

Sew the pieces to the background with tiny blind stitches, beginning with a knot hidden in the seam allowance and ending with one between the applied piece and the backing fabric. Use thread that closely matches the appliqué fabric.

If applied pieces overlap each other, cut the underlying pieces to allow for about 6mm (¼in) overlap. Prepare the fabric pieces as usual, but do not turn under any edges that will be subsequently covered. Pin and tack the underlying pieces in position first and then the overlying ones, making sure that all raw edges are covered. When you come to sew the pieces, make sure that your stitches pass through both the layers of appliqué and the background.

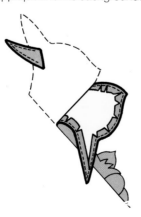

Machine appliqué

Make sure that your machine is in good working order and that you have the appropriate threads for the fabric. You should also check that you have a good supply of the right needles for the fabric or fabrics and that they are new and sharp.

Position the pieces as for hand-sewn work and tack them. Set your machine to a close zigzag stitch and machine round the edge of each shape. To avoid puckers, try to work from the central point of each shape outwards or, if one end of a piece lies under another, work in towards that end so that excess fabric can be tucked under the overlying piece. On curves, raise and lower the foot frequently in order to achieve a smooth line.

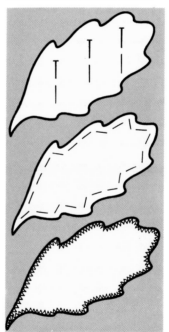

If you set your machine to too close a stitch you may find that it clogs up. In this case, use a more open zigzag and, if necessary, go round the stitches a second time.

You can start and finish with backstitching or, if this is difficult, just pull the threads through to the back and neaten them. When you have finished stitching, remove any tacking stitches that still show and trim away any raw edges or loose threads with sharp embroidery scissors.

Using interfacing

Interfacing is a convenient tool for successful appliqué. If you are using flimsy fabrics or ones that tend to fray, apply a light-weight iron-on interfacing to the fabric before cutting out the motif. You can then treat the interfacing and fabric as one fabric for the purposes of stitching the motif onto the background material.

For quick results use a special fusible webbing. This is made up of an adhesive web with a special paper backing. Iron the webbing onto the wrong side of the motif fabric. After it has cooled, cut out the motif shape, allowing for seam allowances if required. When you have cut out the motif, peel off the paper backing. Place the motif in position on the right side of the background fabric and iron on with a steam iron or a dry iron and damp cloth. This holds the motif firmly while you sew by hand or machine. Remember that if the design has any overlapping motifs, the background motifs must be applied first. Plan the order before you begin ironing.

Padded appliqué

This method produces a textured effect. The motif can be assembled and stitched to a layer of wadding and then attached to the background in one piece.

The choice of padding material is important to ensure that the finished effect is smooth. Use light-weight synthetic wadding for a large motif or interlining fabrics such as domett for a small motif.

Another method of padding appliqué is to slip some synthetic filling between the motif and the background before pinning and sewing. This works well if only one part of the design is padded, giving it emphasis. For example, in a floral motif, the leaves could be slightly padded but not the flowers and stalk. The cushions in the Cushion Miscellany project on page 68 combine appliqué with wadding in various different ways to produce lightly padded or more contoured effects.

COLOURFUL HARMONY

Little finishing touches often make all the difference to a beautiful décor: a few flowers in a vase, echoing the colours of the walls or furnishings, a pretty sofa throw or, in this case, bands of bright, shining satin ribbon, rippling over the damask background of cushions, duvet cover, tablecloth and curtains. Instantly, a scheme which would already have been pretty if the fabrics had been left undecorated becomes something beautiful and much more inspired.

Sizes: cushions 45cm x 26cm (18in x 10¼in); duvet cover 140cm x 200cm (55in x 80in); tablecloth 118cm x 118cm (46½in x 46½in); café curtains to fit your window measurements.

MATERIALS

FOR EACH CUSHION
30cm (⅜yd) of 120cm (48in) wide damask
2cm (¾in) wide ribbon in different colours for border and
appliqué
46.5cm× 27cm (18½in× 10¾in) cushion pad
Matching threads

FOR THE DUVET COVER
2.2m (2½yd) of 120cm (48in) wide yellow damask
2.2m (2½yd) of 120cm (48in) wide pink damask
2cm (¾in) wide ribbon in different colours for appliqué
1m (1yd) of press fastening tape
Matching threads

FOR THE TABLECLOTH
1.2m (1¼yd) of 120cm (48in) wide damask
2cm (¾in) wide ribbon in different
colours for border and appliqué
Matching threads

FOR THE CAFE CURTAINS
120cm (48in) wide damask (see page 53 for quantity)
2cm (¾in) wide ribbon in
different colours for border, appliqué and hanging loops
Matching threads

METHOD

FOR EACH CUSHION
▦ Cut out two pieces of damask each 48cm × 29cm (19¼in × 11½in).

▦ On cushion front arrange 10cm (4in) lengths of ribbon, either running in parallel lines or crossed: the choice is yours. When the arrangement looks good, pin and tack in place. Set your sewing-machine to a close zigzag stitch and test on a small scrap of fabric before stitching. Stitch all around each piece of ribbon, working the long sides in the same direction to avoid wrinkles.

▦ Mark a 1.5cm (⅝in) seam allowance all around cushion front with tacking stitches. Lay a border ribbon around the outer edge, butting the outer edge of the ribbon up against the tacked line and mitring each corner. Begin and end the ribbon behind one mitred corner. Pin, tack and topstitch the ribbon in place.

▦ With right sides together, pin, tack and stitch cushion front to cushion back, leaving an opening centrally in one side. Trim and turn through to the right side.

▦ Insert cushion pad. Turn in opening edges in line with the remainder of the seam and slipstitch together to close.

THE DUVET COVER

▦ One side of the cover is yellow and the other is pink. Both sides are made from four pieces of fabric, two plain and two with ribbon appliqué. From yellow fabric cut two pieces each 103cm × 73cm (41¼in × 27½in) for top (bedhead) quarters and two pieces each 106.5cm × 73cm (42½in × 27½in) for base quarters (the extra length includes an allowance for the fastening). Cut pieces the same size from pink fabric, for the other side of the cover.

▦ Decorate one top and one base section for each side: position two strips of ribbon across the width, spacing them equally from each other and the seamline, and one strip across the length. Pin and tack each strip in place. Set your machine to a close zigzag stitch and test on a spare piece of fabric before stitching. Stitch along all edges of each length of ribbon, stitching across short ends just inside the seamline.

▦ Pin, tack and stitch appliquéd pieces to plain pieces in pairs, along one long edge.

▦ Pin, tack and stitch yellow top pieces to yellow base pieces and pink top pieces to pink base pieces, with appliquéd sections at opposite corners.

▦ Fold a double 2.5cm (1in) wide hem along base edge of each piece; pin, tack and stitch. Place cover pieces with right sides together, matching hem edges; pin, tack and stitch hem edges together for 30cm (12in) in from either side, leaving a central opening.

▦ Pin, tack and stitch press fastener tape into each side of the opening, so that the fasteners match. Stitch across each end of the opening.

▦ Complete the duvet cover with French seams, stitching the sides first and then the top edges.

▦ To complete, stitch ribbon bows to ends of appliqué ribbon at the outer edges of the cover.

THE TABLECLOTH

▦ Turn up a 1cm (⅜in) hem to the right side of the fabric, all around the outer edge. Pin and tack, making neat corners. Position the ribbon around the edge, with the outer edge of the ribbon just covering the raw edges of the fabric. Mitre the corners of the ribbon. Pin, tack and topstitch.

▦ Add other bands of ribbon and 10cm (4in) lengths of ribbon appliqué in the same way as for the cushion covers.

THE CAFE CURTAIN

▦ Measure the height of your window and decide how deep you wish your finished curtain to be: it could cover only half the window, or the full length, allowing for a gap at the top for loops. Cut fabric to the desired finished depth plus 14cm (5½in), and to the pole width plus 4cm (1½in) for each side hem.

▦ Turn under a double 2cm (¾in) hem at both side edges and pin. Turn under and pin a double 5cm (2in) hem at the lower edge and a double 2cm (¾in) hem at the top. Mitre all corners, then stitch hems all around curtain.

▦ Position a border of ribbon all around the curtain, 2.5cm (1in) from outer edge, mitring the corners. Position ribbon ends underneath a mitred corner. Pin, tack and topstitch in place, stitching along both edges.

▦ Position inner rows of ribbon in two different colours and stitch in the same way. Add lengths of appliquéd ribbon, as for cushions.

▦ Work with two different colours of ribbon to provide the hanging loops along the top edge; attach the first ribbon behind the outer edge. Tack along the back of the curtain at 8cm (3¼in) intervals, forming 4cm (1½in) loops as shown. Pin the folded ribbon in place at the back. Stitch in place.

▦ Repeat with the second coloured ribbon, spacing loops of the same size centrally between the first set.

▦ Tie the two ends together at the side. Slide the curtain onto the pole.

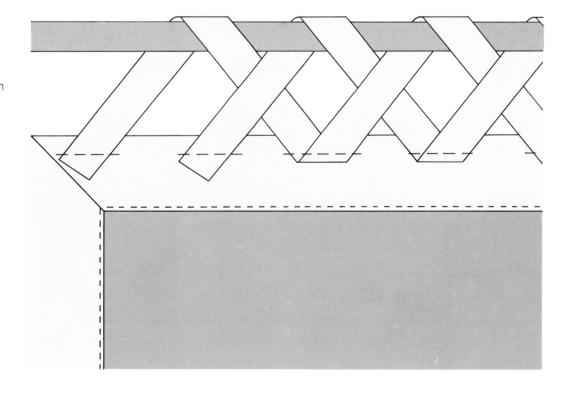

SYMPHONY IN NEUTRALS

The subtly varied shapes of this small cloth, emphasized by a restrained use of textured neutrals, are derived from the fabrics used for *furoshiki*, the square cloths in which the Japanese traditionally wrap gifts. Like so many other aspects of Japanese life, *furoshiki* are an art form in themselves, and this small cloth could be used either as a wall hanging or to grace the centre of a small occasional table.

MATERIALS

70cm (28in) square of fine white linen for the base fabric
80cm (⅞yd) of 90cm (36in) wide ecru wild silk for the border and appliqué

Oddments of black and white linens for the appliqué
Matching threads

METHOD

▦ Scale up the patterns for the motifs and cut out the shapes from thin card or tracing paper.

▦ Mark each pattern out on the right side of the appropriate fabric and add a 6mm (¼in) allowance all round. Cut out beyond the seam allowance and then staystitch round each motif, stitching within the seam allowance and just outside the marked foldline. Cut out each motif along the outer line.

▦ Fold the seam allowance to the wrong side all round each piece, pinning and then tacking. To form smooth curves, take notches out of the seam allowance on outward-facing curves and make clips up to the foldline on inward-facing curves.

▦ When the shapes are prepared, pin them to the background, as shown, and tack them vertically in place. Where shapes overlap each other, pin, tack and stitch the bottom layer first, and then apply the next layer on top of the first. Use matching thread to sew each piece in place with small, neat slipstitches.

▦ When the appliqué is finished, remove tacking stitches. Take the remaining ecru silk and cut four border strips 10cm (4in) deep, cutting across the full 90cm (36in) width of the fabric.

▦ Taking a 1cm (⅜in) seam, attach two side strips, stopping 1cm (⅜in) short of the edge at each corner. Next attach the top and bottom strips in the same way, so that they meet exactly at the corners of the appliquéd piece and the ends are left free. Fold the ends of the side strips diagonally under to make mitred corners and sew them down by hand. Neaten.

▦ Trim across the corners and finish the border with a 1cm (⅜in) double hem.

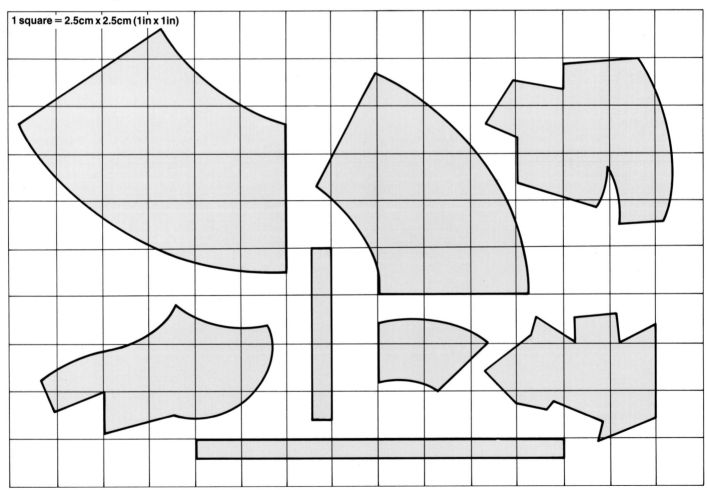

1 square = 2.5cm x 2.5cm (1in x 1in)

LARGER THAN LIFE

This eccentric tablecloth, decorated with a medley of outsize fruits, mugs and fans (to help you to keep cool on hot summer days) is guaranteed to put a keen edge on your appetite. If you enjoy hand sewing, you can appliqué the various motifs to the background fabric by hand, but if not, then they can easily be applied with a machine zigzag stitch. If you are really lucky you might be able to find a fabric with a pattern close to that of your china, to give the appliquéd mugs a trompe l'oeil effect.

Size: 202cm × 148cm (80½in × 59in).

MATERIALS

1.6m (1⅞yd) of 120cm (48in) wide plain blue fabric
1.6m (1⅞yd) of 115cm (45in) wide black and white check fabric
Assortment of different coloured, plain and printed fabrics for appliqué
Oddments of broderie anglaise, broderie anglaise edging and braid for appliqué
Green embroidery cotton
Yellow and pink fabric paints
Matching thread

METHOD

▦ From check fabric cut out two pieces, each 160cm by 50cm (64in by 20in).

▦ Draw up the patterns for the motifs from the diagram. Cut out eight lemons from plain yellow fabric, three apples and three plums from plain green fabric. From plain orange fabric cut out seven 20cm (8in) diameter circles, for oranges. Cut out three large and four small strawberries from plain red fabric with stalks from plain green. When pinning them to the background fabric, overlay the stalks on top of the strawberries and zigzag stitch in place. Embroider seeds in bullion knots, as shown.

▦ Paint over the tops of the strawberries with yellow or pink paint, and fix according to manufacturer's instructions.

▦ From printed fabric cut out three mugs. Position braid round mug, as shown; pin, tack and zigzag stitch in place. From plain blue fabric cut out a large flower motif for each mug. Appliqué to each mug, as before.

▦ Make up two fans: cut out from printed fabric, then lay bands of broderie anglaise or second print fabric over the fan and zigzag stitch in place. Pin and tack broderie anglaise edging behind the curved outer edge of broderie anglaise fan.

▦ Trim blue fabric to 160cm x 120cm (64in x 48in). Lay it right side up on a flat surface and position all the motifs following the diagram, overlapping the outer edges where shown. Pin and tack them in place close to the outer edge. Zigzag stitch around each motif, adding stalks to the apples.

▦ Appliqué shapes to each piece of check fabric in the same way following the diagram for positions.

▦ Pin, tack and stitch check fabric strips to either side of blue fabric with flat fell seams.

▦ Turn under a 6cm (2½in) hem all around outer edge, tuck under 1cm (⅜in), mitring the corners. Pin, tack and stitch hem in place.

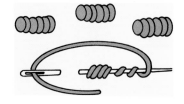

56

1 square = 5cm x 5cm (2in x 2in)

Raw edges will be covered by the stitching, but the pieces must first be tacked to the background fabric with the stitches running all around, fairly close to the edge. When machining the stalks, work up to each point, then raise the presser foot while the needle is in the down position and turn the fabric.

1 square = 20cm x 20cm (8in x 8in)

INSTANT SEATING

The elegant contrast between sober navy and pure white gives these simple box cushions an air of great style, but they are also extremely comfortable, with two layers of foam, one on top of the other. Use them for sitting or just for lounging about, tucking them away in a corner when you don't need them, and when you want to wash the white covers you simply untie the knots and lift them off.

Size: 30cm (12in) high and 65cm (26in) square.

MATERIALS

Two 65cm × 65cm (26in × 26in) blocks of 15cm (6in) deep foam	12.5m (13¾yd) or 9.3m (10¼yd) of 2.5cm (1in) wide navy tape (amount varies according to
1.2m (1⅜yd) of 140cm (56in) wide white woven fabric	whether tape is stitched in double or single lines)
1.7m (1⅞yd) of 115cm (45in) wide navy woven fabric	Matching threads

METHOD

▦ For the base cushion, cut two pieces each 68cm × 68cm (27¼in × 27¼in) from navy fabric, and four side gusset pieces, each 68cm × 18cm (27¼in × 7¼in).

▦ The tapes on the top cover are formed either in two double lines running each way or with three evenly spaced strands running each way. Cut 17cm (6¾in) lengths of tape and stitch them to side gusset pieces of base to correspond with chosen pattern for top: either four or three for each side, and positioned 9cm (3½in) up from the lower edge.

▦ Taking 1.5cm (⅝in) seam allowances, pin, tack and stitch gusset pieces into a ring, beginning and ending stitching 1.5cm (⅝in) from ends of each seam.

▦ Pin, tack and stitch gusset to base cushion piece, matching seams to corners. Pin, tack and stitch top cushion piece to opposite edge of gusset in the same way, but leaving an opening of one side and the first 7.5cm (3in) of the adjoining sides. Trim and turn cover to the right side. Insert foam; turn in the raw edges in line with the remainder of the seam and slipstitch together to close.

▦ For top cover, cut 120cm × 120cm (48in × 48in) of white fabric. Centre the fabric over the second foam block and mark the corners with pins.

▦ Position strips of tape across the fabric, either with two double lines running each way or with three evenly spaced strands running each way. Place second block over first and fabric over both to check that top tapes will

join neatly and accurately with bottom tapes. The strips should be 8.5cm (3½in) longer than the fabric at either end. Pin and stitch the tapes in position, stitching close to the edge down each side and stopping 6.5cm (2½in) short of the raw edge of the fabric at either end, leaving 15cm (6in) free to form ties.

▦ Make a 2cm (¾in) wide buttonhole in the cover 13mm (½in) below the stitching at end of each tape.

▦ Stack uncovered foam block on top of covered foam, matching edges. Place fabric, wrong side out, centrally over the foam blocks and pin darts at each corner so that the cover fits smoothly over the blocks. Work from top corners downwards and leave darts unpinned for the last 6.5cm (2½in) from base edge.

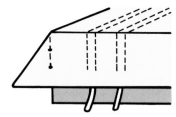

▦ Remove cover; pin, tack and stitch darts up to 6.5cm (2½in) from base edge.

▦ Press darts, including unstitched ends. Cut along foldline, and press darts open. Neaten raw edges and slipstitch allowances neatly in place at the back of the cover.

▦ Turn up a 4cm (1½in) hem around lower edge of top cover and stitch.

▦ Replace cover on blocks; thread lower tapes through buttonholes and tie them to the upper tapes.

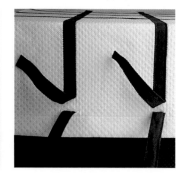

A ROSE IS A ROSE

Turn an uninteresting view into something with a hint of magic and suspense with this light, airy blind. The secret lies in the clear plastic window set into white satin; for windows within windows, like boxes within boxes, convey a feeling of mystery and the excitement of discovery. In this case, the window has its own hidden secret, for the decoration of corded scrollwork with which it is covered is not a random tangle, as might at first appear, but the word 'rose', repeated over and over again.

Size: this can be adjusted to individual requirements; the central plastic window measures 17.5cm×15cm (7in×6in).

MATERIALS

White satin – to your measurements (see below)	*Fabric adhesive*
19.5cm × 17cm (7¾in × 6¾in) sheet of transparent plastic	*Matching thread*
4m (4½yd) of flat white cord	*Length of 2.5cm (1in) diameter dowel to fit across window, plus fixing brackets*

METHOD

▦ Measure the window and cut out satin to this size, adding 14cm (5½in) to the length for top casing and base hem and 4cm (1½in) to the width for side hems.

▦ Turn under double 1cm (⅜in) wide hem down both side edges and along base edge, forming neat base corners. Pin, tack and stitch hems in place.

▦ For top casing turn under 1cm (⅜in), then a further 11cm (4⅜in); pin, tack and stitch across blind.

▦ Starch and iron the satin. Mark the centre lengthways.

▦ Mark, with tacking stitches, a 17.5cm × 15cm (7in × 6in) window centrally on blind, about two thirds up from base edge. Cut out a central section 15.5cm × 13cm (6¼in × 5¼in) from inside the marked rectangle and discard. Snip into the corners up to the tacking stitches; turn back the edges along the tacked lines, and carefully stick them to the wrong side, removing the tacking stitches as you work.

▦ Following the design, stick the cord over one side of the plastic

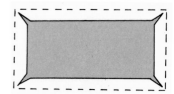

sheet in loops, being careful not to spread adhesive on the clear plastic areas. Leave to dry.

▦ Position the plastic centrally behind the window and stick in place to turned-back edges of fabric. If necessary, topstitch round edge of window.

▦ Slide dowel through top casing and hang blind.

SUNSHINE AND SHADOW

Two simple but elegant design ideas for quick, stylish curtains, using nothing more complicated than squares. The plastic curtain with its square appliquéd pockets containing black and white or multicoloured strands of cotton will hide a dull view but let the sunshine flood into your room. The shadow-design curtains are made from pure white cotton scattered with grey squares stitched on top of black sateen ones, slightly staggered to give the shadow effect. They are made in three panels to allow the air to circulate and to create the perfect cool, calm setting for a holiday home.

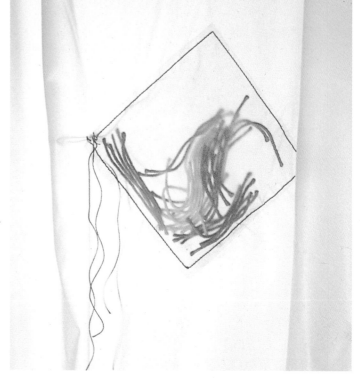

MATERIALS

SUNSHINE CURTAIN
Shower curtaining
Transparent plastic for the squares
Shiny mercerized cotton in a variety of colours
Adhesive tape
Sewing thread in a variety of colours

SHADOW CURTAINS
Plain white cotton fabric for curtains
Oddment of black sateen
Oddment of grey flannelette
Matching threads

METHOD

SUNSHINE CURTAIN

▦ Make up the curtain to the desired size, with double 1cm (⅜in) side hems and a double 4cm (1½in) base hem. At the top, either make a cased heading or attach a fine heading tape.

▦ For the border, cut out 7cm (3in) squares of plastic and for the central motifs, 9cm (3½in) squares.

▦ Position each square in turn on the curtain and hold in place with small amounts of adhesive tape. Zigzag stitch three sides, using two contrasting threads, one for the top and one in the bobbin. Insert strands of mercerized cotton and close the remaining side of each square.

SHADOW CURTAINS

▦ Make up three curtain panels to the correct size, with double 1cm (⅜in) side hems and a double 4cm (1½in) base hem. At the top, either make a cased heading or attach a fine heading tape.

▦ Decide on the size of the appliqué squares: 10cm (4in) is a good size. Make a template from thin card and mark out a sufficient number of squares on the grey and black fabrics. For each square, use the template to mark the foldline on the wrong side of the fabric, then add a 6mm (¼in) seam allowance all round.

▦ Cut out each square along the outer marked line and turn the seam allowance to the wrong side, cutting across each corner point and mitring the corners to reduce bulk. Pin and tack all round each square.

▦ Position the black squares on each curtain and tack them vertically in place. Set your machine to a medium-length stitch and, with matching thread, stitch around the outer edge of each square.

▦ Remove the tacking stitches, then position a grey square to overlap each black one and repeat the process, again using matching thread.

▦ When all the stitching is complete, remove the remaining tacking stitches and pull the ends through to the wrong side. Fasten them through the stitching at the back or, alternatively, knot them in pairs and cut off the ends.

WINDOW CHIC

The different sheens and textures of this complex appliqué blind provide interest and variety while allowing ample daylight to filter through in a subtle range of nuances and tones. Made with a combination of machine appliqué and embroidery, together with cutwork, it is not the sort of thing which a complete beginner can run up in an evening, but if you have a certain degree of skill and confidence, the result will be very rewarding, and very chic.

Finished size: 60cm (24in) wide × 90cm (36in) long

MATERIALS

1.1m (1¼yd) each of 122cm (48in) wide white sateen and white cotton net	Shiny white machine embroidery thread
50cm (⅝yd) square of white satin	Matching thread
	Length of dowel or curtain pole, plus hanging hooks

METHOD

▦ Fix hooks on either side of window to hold pole.

▦ From sateen, cut one piece 110cm × 62cm (43in × 24½in). Cut a piece of cotton net the same size and place the two with right sides together and pin and tack down one (long) side. Machine, taking 1cm (⅜in) allowance. Repeat for other side, this time pulling net over to overlap raw edge of sateen by 6mm (¼in).

▦ Turn right side out and press side hems. Working across and vertically, tack the fabrics together at 10cm (4in) intervals.

▦ Scale up the three appliqué motifs from the diagram and cut the appropriate numbers from white satin. Take a long rule and a sharp, light-coloured pencil and lightly draw in the vertical and horizontal lines, using the diagram as a guide and starting 25cm (10in) up from the base edge.

▦ Pin and tack the motifs in position then, using a close zigzag stitch, carefully stitch round each piece. With the same stitch, complete the remaining lines of the design, stitching up to the top edge of the blind. After stitching, pull all loose threads to the wrong side and fasten off.

▦ Using sharp-pointed scissors, carefully cut out the sateen only from areas indicated on the diagram, to reveal the net.

▦ At the base, turn up 1cm (⅜in) and then 4cm (1½in) to form a hem.

▦ Turn 1cm (⅜in) then 12cm (5in) to wrong side at top of blind, to form a casing. Pin, tack and stitch across. Insert dowel/pole and hang on hooks at either side of window.

ROLLER BLIND

▦ Position brackets on each side of the window with pin hole on the right and square bracket on the left. Trim roller to fit – hammer on end cap with pin.

▦ Turn down top edge for 1.5cm (⅝in) to right side. Lay roller across blind top; with folded edge to marked edge on roller; hammer tacks in place along folded edge.

▦ At the base turn up 1cm (⅜in) and then 4cm (1½in) to form a casing; pin, tack and stitch one end and across the casing. Trim lath to 1.5cm (⅝in) shorter than the casing. Slide lath into casing; slipstitch open end to close. Make up a cord pull and fasten cord holder centrally to wrong side of lath casing.

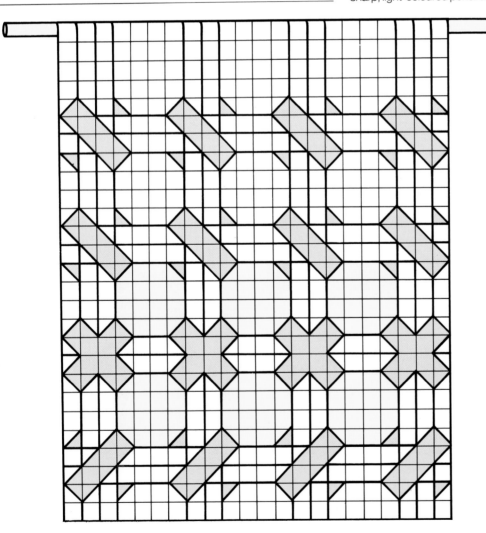

1 square = 2.5cm × 2.5cm (1in × 1in)

▨ satin appliqué motifs

▧ sateen cutouts

— zigzag stitching lines

the sophisticated elegance of white-on-white

CUSHION MISCELLANY

There is something for everyone in this selection of cushions, which ranges from the realistic fun of the hen and nest to the elegant sophistication of ecru-on-black appliqué or the subtly textured effect of the circular cushion, but all are worked with a machine zigzag stitch. The hen is constructed rather like a tea cosy and is designed to hold bib and wiper, while the nest is securely fastened with ribbons tied spartan fashion. The ecru leaf pattern was inspired by Japanese art and is lightly padded, and the veined pattern of the circular cushion could similarly be worked over a thin layer of wadding to give a slight relief effect.

MATERIALS

THE HEN

1m (1yd) of 90cm (36in) wide chestnut-coloured cotton fabric
40cm × 80cm (16in × 32in) of medium-weight polyester wadding

Scraps of felt or cotton in yellow, red and beige
Two buttons for eyes
Dressmakers' pattern paper
Dressmakers' carbon paper
Matching threads

THE NEST

40cm (½yd) of 90cm (36in) wide turquoise cotton fabric
15cm (6in) of 90cm (36in) wide ecru cotton fabric
50cm (20in) square of light-weight wadding
4.5m (5yd) of 1cm (⅜in) wide ribbon

Dressmakers' pattern paper
Dressmakers' carbon paper
Matching and contrasting threads
36cm (14in) cushion pad

LEAF CUSHION

1m (1yd) of 90cm (36in) wide black sateen
40cm (½yd) of 90cm (36in) wide ecru sateen
Suitable filling for the motif

Dressmakers' pattern paper
Dressmakers' carbon paper
Matching threads
30cm (12in) cushion pad

CIRCULAR CUSHION

50cm (⅝yd) of 90cm (36in) wide ecru cotton fabric
50cm (⅝yd) of 100cm (40in) wide light-weight polyester wadding (optional)

Pencil or tailors' chalk
36cm (14in) diameter circle of 4cm (1½in) thick foam

METHOD

THE HEN

▦ Draw up the patterns for the hen, beak, comb and wattle from the diagram, marking in the feather lines. Cut out four hen shapes, adding a 1.5cm (⅝in) seam allowance. Mark design on right side of one pair.

▦ From beige fabric cut out two 2.5cm (1in) diameter circles for cheeks. Place each cheek on one of a pair of hen shapes; pin, tack and zigzag stitch cheeks in place. Stitch on a button for each eye.

▦ Place a layer of wadding behind two hen shapes and, using colours shown, work

68

feathers in a close zigzag stitch on a sewing machine. It may help if you back the wadding with tissue paper to be pulled away after machining.

▥ Place red comb and wattle pieces in pairs with wrong sides together; pin, tack and zigzag stitch together round the outer edge. Repeat to make up beak from yellow fabric.

▥ Place hen shapes with right sides together. Pin, tack and stitch together, taking a 1.5cm (⅝in) seam allowance. Leave base open. Turn right side out. Pin and tack the prepared comb, wattle and beak pieces in position on the front of the hen. Attach to the head with close machine zigzag stitch.

▥ Stitch the two remaining hen shapes together, again leaving base open. Insert into decorated hen. Turn edges in to meet each other round base opening: pin, tack and topstitch close to edge.

THE NEST

▥ Draw up the pattern from the diagram, marking in straw lines.

▥ From turquoise fabric cut out two cushion pieces, each 39cm (15¼in) square. Cut a piece of wadding the same size.

▥ Transfer the design to one cushion piece and pin and tack wadding behind it. Using a close zigzag stitch, work in the straw lines in lime and blue.

▥ From ecru cotton fabric cut out three eggs. Repeat, to cut eggs from wadding. Pin and tack to wrong side of fabric eggs. Place eggs in the centre of the cushion, overlapping each other. Pin, tack and zigzag stitch.

▥ Place cushion pieces with right sides together, raw edges matching; pin, tack and stitch together all round, leaving an opening in the centre of one side, for turning. Trim and turn to right side. Insert cushion pad. Turn in opening edges and slipstitch together to close.

▥ Cut ribbon into two 60cm (24in) lengths and two 160cm (64in) lengths. Handstitch the centre of each length to each corner, with large ties placed at the front.

1 square = 2.5cm x 2.5cm (1in x 1in)

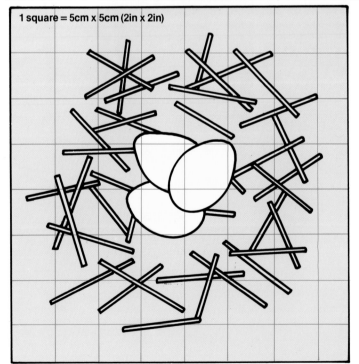

1 square = 5cm x 5cm (2in x 2in)

CIRCULAR CUSHION

▥ From fabric cut out two 39cm (15¼in) diameter circles. For the gusset, measure round the cushion 1.5cm (⅝in) in from the edge and cut one piece to this length plus 3cm (1¼in) seam allowance and 7cm (2¾in) wide.

▥ If using wadding, cut one circle and one gusset, without seam allowances, from wadding, and pin and tack to back of one fabric circle and gusset.

▥ Staystitch all round the circles, 1.5cm (⅝in) from the outer edge. Snip into the seam allowance up to the stitching. With right sides together, pin, tack and stitch the gusset together into a ring. Position gusset round one circle (if using wadding, pin to wadded circle). Pin, tack and stitch together round line of stay-stitching.

▥ Mark in lines for decorative stitching across the cushion and gusset with a pencil or tailors'

1 square = 5cm x 5cm (2in x 2in)

THE LEAF CUSHION

▦ Draw up the design from the diagram, including all the design lines.

▦ From black sateen cut out two pieces each 33cm (13¼in) square. From ecru sateen cut out one leaf arrangement and transfer design lines to the motif.

▦ Position the leaf arrangement centrally on one cushion piece. Using matching thread, pin and tack round, taking small stitches and adding a small amount of filling as you work. When

complete, zigzag stitch round the design. Then zigzag stitch the design lines using black thread.

▦ Place the two cushion cover pieces with right sides together; pin, tack and stitch together all round, leaving a central opening in one side. Trim and turn to right side. Insert cushion pad; turn in opening edges and slipstitch together to close.

chalk. Work a tight zigzag stitch over the marked decorative lines.

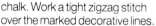

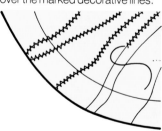

▦ Place second cushion cover piece to opposite edge of gusset with right sides together. Pin, tack and stitch together, leaving an opening. Trim and turn to right side. Insert foam; turn in opening edges in line with the remainder of the seam; slipstitch together to close.

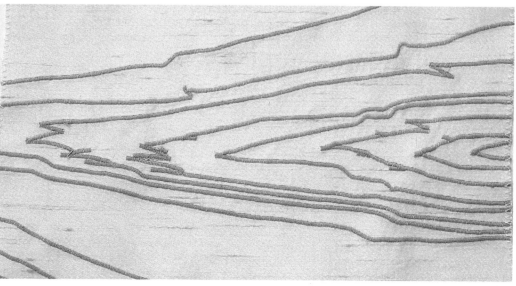

MEXICAN HEATWAVE

In addition to hot sun and even hotter food, Mexico is well known for its bold, eye-catching art, alive with colourful flowers, brilliant birds and strange, fierce gods. These cushion covers, inspired by elaborate Mexican paper cut-outs, are guaranteed to bring you a touch of Latin American sunshine even in the depths of winter.

Size: to fit cushion pads measuring 40cm × 30cm (16in × 12in)

MATERIALS

For each cover:	*Dressmakers' pattern paper*
50cm (⅝yd) of 90cm (36in) wide white linen	*Marking pen*
	30cm (12in) zip
45cm × 35cm (18in × 14in) of felt in pink, yellow or blue	*Matching threads*
	Masking tape

METHOD

▦ For cushion front, cut out a piece of linen 43cm × 33cm (17¼in × 13¼in).

▦ Scale up the chosen design on dressmakers' pattern paper then carefully cut out the shaded area from the diagram. You can do this with good paper scissors, but it will be easier to cut accurately if you tape the design down to a good cutting surface, to hold it steady, and use a craft knife.

▦ Place the pattern centrally on the felt and tape the corners to hold it steady, then tape the edges of the felt to your worktop. Carefully mark out the design using a marking pen.

▦ Using a pair of sharp-pointed scissors, cut out the design.

▦ Centre the felt on the cushion front. Pin and tack it in place, taking care not to stretch it. Using matching thread, neatly slipstitch round all the cut-out sections and the edge.

▦ For the cushion back, cut a piece of fabric 43cm × 36cm (17¼in × 14½in). Cut in half lengthways across the centre. With right sides together and taking a 1.5cm (⅝in) seam allowance, pin, tack and stitch 6.5cm (2½in) in from either side. Tack remainder of seam and position zip centrally behind the tacked section. Pin, tack and stitch zip in place. Open zip.

▦ Place cushion front to cushion back, right sides together. Pin, tack and stitch together all round, just beyond outer edge of felt. Trim and neaten seam. Turn to right side through zip. Insert cushion pad and close zip.

▦ Repeat this method to make the remaining cushion covers, using the two other colours.

CUT-OUT DESIGN

If the designs given here are not suited to your decor, you can easily make your own patterns using the method shown here, which is based on the elaborate style of appliqué known as Hawaiian. The main difference between designs produced by this method and the Mexican patterns given here is that the Hawaiian method produces symmetrical shapes radiating from a central point, which are placed on a square or circular background.

Take a square piece of paper and fold it in half, making sure that the edges meet exactly.

Take the paper and fold it in half again, once more checking that the corners and edges meet neatly.

Fold the paper again, this time diagonally, folding it so that all the folded edges lie on one short side of the diagonal fold and all the cut edges lie on the other short side.

Draw a design on the folded paper, as shown, making sure that the design is connected along the diagonal and the short folded edges.

Cut out along the outline(s) and then unfold the design. Make several patterns before choosing the most attractive and using it as a paper template to mark your felt.

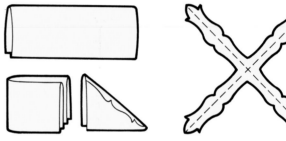

1 square = 10cm x 10cm (4in x 4in)

1 square = 10cm x 10cm (4in x 4in)

1 square = 10cm x 10cm (4in x 4in)

If you do not want to make a cushion cover, you could use one of these designs to make a bright, attractive wall hanging. Make casings at the top and bottom and slot thin strips of wood or bamboo through to hold it flat and provide a hanger.

Sew a felt design to a cloth bag, for an unusual and attractive shoulder bag with an ethnic flavour or, for a more practical and everyday shopping bag, make a vinyl cut-out and stick it in place.

Brighten up the lunch table with appliquéd place mats – the felt will help to protect the table from hot plates.

FOREST TRACK

This table runner, made of matting embellished with an appliquéd satin design of leaves and acorns, would make the perfect accompaniment to an autumnal arrangement of flame- and copper-coloured leaves, or dried flowers and seed heads, or to bowls of nuts or russet apples. We have used fusible webbing to stick the design to the mat ready for sewing, but it could equally well be tacked in place and then trimmed after sewing.

Finished size: 120cm × 40cm (48in × 16in)

MATERIALS

One table runner made of fine matting, 120cm × 40cm (48in × 16in) – if you cannot find a mat of the correct size or fine enough to take the embroidery, use hessian, making a narrow hem down the long sides

Piece of khaki green sateen 20cm × 90cm (8in × 36in)
Coats machine embroidery thread in brown, yellow and greens
One skein of DMC special in 307
Dressmakers' carbon paper
Dressmakers' pattern paper
Fusible webbing

METHOD

▦ Draw up the design from the diagram. Mark the design on one side of the fusible webbing. Cut out outside the outline. Fuse on to the wrong side of sateen fabric. Carefully cut out round the marked outline.

▦ Remove backing and position along one short edge of runner, as shown in diagram and picture, and pin in place. Press in position. Remove pins and press in place again, this time over a damp cloth.

▦ Test the zigzag stitch on the machine and select length and width. Using threads as shown, stitch round each leaf, then stitch veins, twigs and acorns. Embroider inside the acorns in satin stitch.

▦ Using sharp-pointed scissors, carefully cut out enclosed portions and along outlines of leaves overlapping edge of runner.

▦ Repeat to decorate the opposite end of the runner in the same way.

1 square = 5cm x 5cm (2in x 2in)

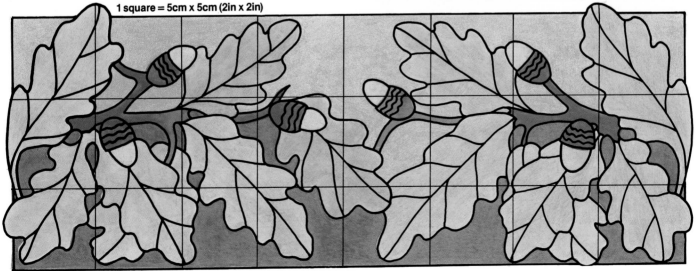

FRUITY LINEN

An extravagant display of fruit spills out across the sheet and is echoed at the corner of the pillowcases to make a luxurious, exotic and gently crazy set of bed linen. The motifs are embroidered after being appliquéd on to plain sheets –, white, peach or yellow would all make good background colours. If you normally use a duvet, buy sheeting and work the appliqué, then make the sheeting into a duvet cover, following the instructions given on page 52.

MATERIALS

Cotton fabric in assorted colours for appliqué	Tracing paper
Dressmakers' pattern paper	Matching threads
	Cotton sheet and pillowcases

METHOD

▦ Draw up the pattern from the diagrams, butting together the edges marked to give the continuous design. Trace off each motif of the design to form a

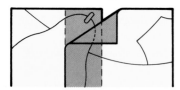

template. Where edges are covered by the next motif, simply straighten the line that will be underneath. Cut out each tracing paper motif.

▦ Pin each template in turn on the right side of the chosen fabric. Mark round the template. Remove the template and cut out, leaving a margin all round of at least 1 cm (⅜in).

▦ Position the first motif in place on the sheet, as shown in the picture. Pin and tack in place. In

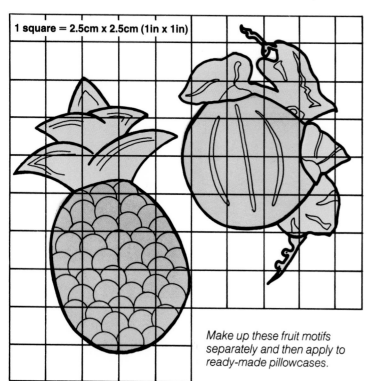

1 square = 2.5cm x 2.5cm (1in x 1in)

Make up these fruit motifs separately and then apply to ready-made pillowcases.

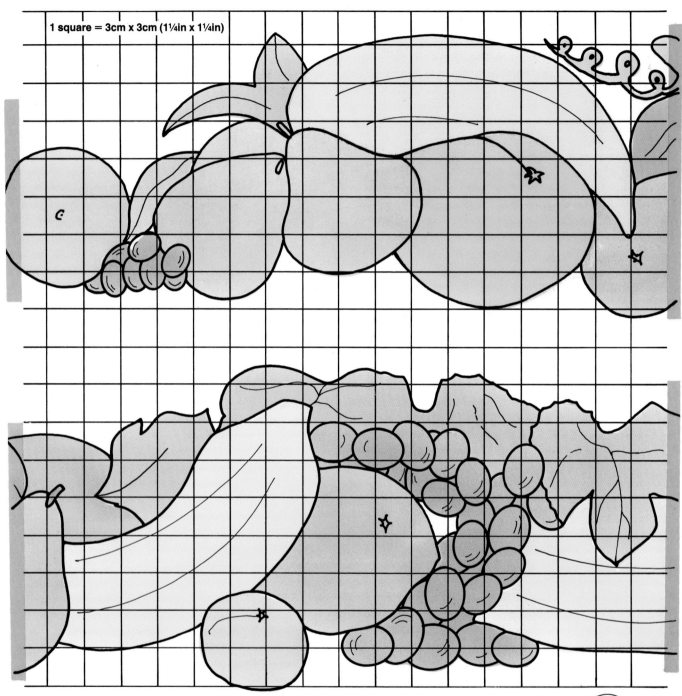

1 square = 3cm x 3cm (1¼in x 1¼in)

the case of the larger pieces it is advisable to tack vertically across the motif as well as round the outer edge.

▦ With a straight running stitch, stitch in place along the marked outline.

▦ Using a pair of sharp-pointed scissors, trim away excess fabric from the motif, as close to the stitching as possible. Set the

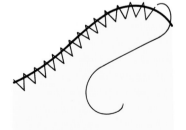

sewing machine to a close zigzag stitch and stitch over the raw edges covering the straight stitching and keeping the stitching even. After stitching, pull all the threads to the wrong side and fasten off securely.

▦ Repeat, to stitch each appliqué in place, overlapping where shown. Add lines of zigzag stitching for ridges and veins.

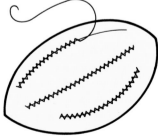

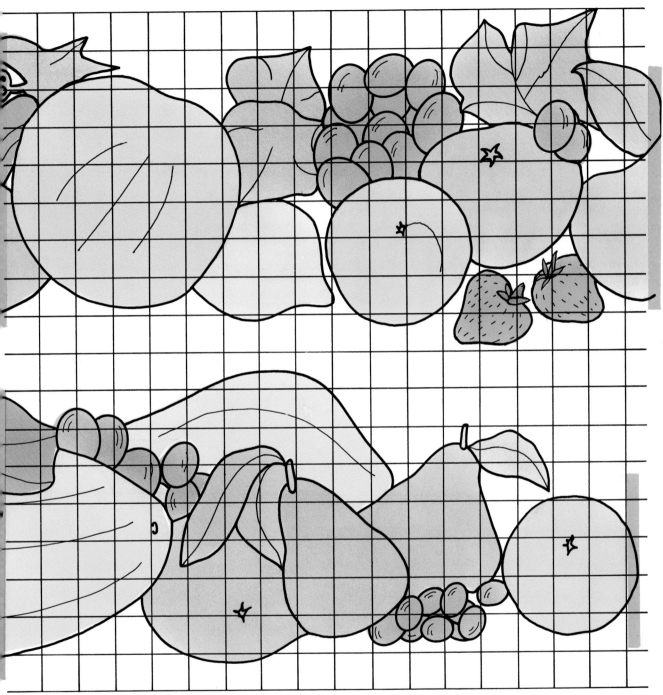

For the pillowcases, trace off one fruit and leaf motif and mark on the appropriate fabrics. Tack the motif pieces in position on a piece of backing fabric, using the same fabric as the pillow-case, if possible. Zigzag stitch all round, adding fruit and leaf details. Trim.

Position the motif in one corner of the pillowcase, overlapping the edges. Stitch in place by hand: either backstitch around inner line of zigzag stitching, or oversew with slanting stitches following the zigzag stitches.

CAT AND MOUSE GAME

Can Miss Mouse find her way through the maze and arrive safely at the birthday party without falling into Mistress Cat's claws, or will her human friend have to help her? This enchanting duvet, with its appliquéd cat and maze and embroidered mice, will keep a little child happily absorbed for ages. The size given would fit a cot duvet, but you could easily enlarge the design and work it on a bigger cover.

Finished size: 120cm × 100cm (47in × 39in)

MATERIALS

1.3m (1½yd) of 228cm (90in) wide straw-coloured sheeting
2cm (¾in) wide cotton tape: 70cm (¾yd) of dark blue, 2m (2¼yd) of medium blue, 3m (3½yd) of pale blue, 2m (2¼yd) of pale green, 1.6m (1¾yd) of medium green, 1.2m (1⅓yd) of pale pink, 1m (1yd) of medium pink, 70cm (28in) of dark pink and oddment of golden yellow for ball.

DMC coton mouliné special in white, black, grey 415, pink 602, pink 603, pink 604, pink 605, pink 818, brown 434, green 910, green 369 and yellow 743
Touch and close spots
Scrap of plain white cotton fabric
Dressmakers' carbon paper
Tracing paper
Matching threads

METHOD

▦ Cut out two pieces of sheeting, each measuring 126.5cm × 103cm (50in × 40½in). Fold a double 2.5cm (1in) wide hem along base edge of each piece, then pin, tack and stitch.

▦ Mark the centre both ways on top cover piece. Following the diagram for colours, position lengths of tape round the centre point. Pin and tack in place, mitring the corners, to make the first square 16cm × 16cm (6½in × 6½in). The remaining squares are successively 3cm (1¼in) further out. Where tapes meet and at ends, tuck under raw edges for 6mm (¼in) to neaten.

▦ When all the tape is in position, topstitch in place, close to edges on both sides of the tape.

▦ Trace off the cat motif and mark it on the white cotton. Cut out, leaving 1.5cm (⅝in) allowance all round. On the outward-facing (convex) curves, make a line of small running stitches, leaving the ends free and sewing just outside the marked line.

▦ Trim seam allowance down to 6mm (¼in) then turn it under and tack all round, pulling up the gathering thread slightly and taking out notches, so that the curve lies smooth. Pin the cat in position on cover and tack it in place around the edge, just in from the fold, then stitch it in place with small, neat slipstitches. Using

80

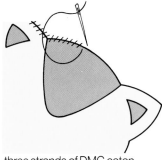

three strands of DMC coton, outline the areas to be embroidered with chainstitch, then fill in with long and short stitch.

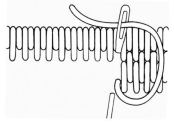

▦ Trace off the mice and table motifs and, using dressmakers' carbon paper, mark them on cover as shown in diagram. Using three strands of DMC coton, embroider, following the diagram for colours.

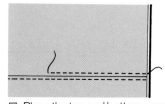

▦ Place the top and bottom cover pieces with right sides together, stitch alongside base hem, leaving a central opening of 60cm (24in).
▦ Place the pieces with wrong sides together and stitch round top and side edges, 1cm (⅝in) in from edge. Trim close to seamline; turn wrong side out and press, then stitch again, 6mm (¼in) from fold, enclosing first seam.
▦ Turn cover right side out and stitch touch and close spots, equally spaced on both sides of opening.

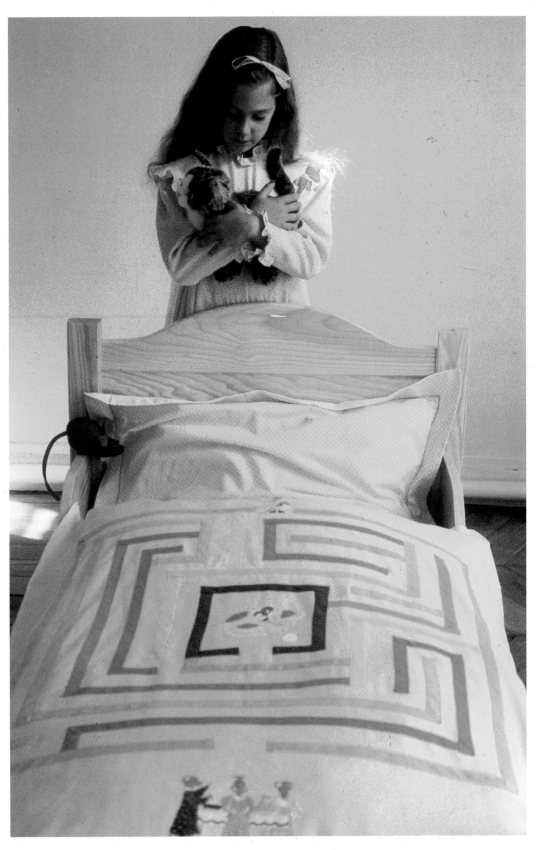

CAT AND MOUSE GAME

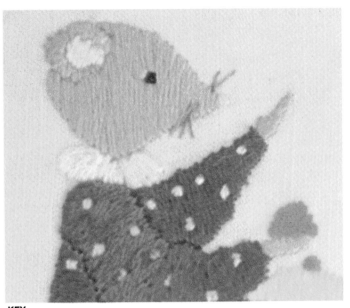

KEY
A White
B Black
C Grey 415
D Pink 602
E Pink 603
F Pink 604

G Pink 605
H Pink 818
I Brown 434
J Green 910
K Green 369
L Yellow 743

HOARDING SQUIRRELS

What child would be able to resist these appliquéd and embroidered squirrels? They can be used to decorate plain bed linen, or a wall hanging. The wall hanging can be made up with patch pockets for storing slippers, gloves or papers and the squirrels can be appliquéd to the edge of the pockets so that they appear to be storing nuts there themselves.

MATERIALS

Oddments of dark brown and
  printed fabrics
One skein of DMC embroidery
  silk in each of the following
  colours: white, pink 3689,

grey 413, dark brown 801, 434
  and 738, and green 732
Tracing paper
Dressmakers' carbon paper
Matching threads

METHOD

▦ Scale up the chosen motifs on to tracing paper and mark on the appliqué fabrics (if you are making the jacketed squirrel, cut out a whole body and put the jacket on top). Add a 6mm (¼in) seam allowance round each motif and cut out, leaving a further 6mm (¼in) beyond the outer line.

▦ Staystitch round each motif, just outside the inner line, then cut along the outer line. Clipping into curves and cutting across at the corners, turn under the allowance all round and tack.

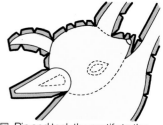

▦ Pin and tack the motifs to the background. Slipstitch each piece in place by hand.

▦ Embroider the remaining details of the animals and nuts, using straight stitch and stem stitch. Halve the embroidery skein when stitching muzzle, eyes, whiskers and claws.

QUILTING

BASIC ESSENTIALS

Quilting changes the texture of fabric, creating shadows and raised areas with lines of tiny stitches. It is a way of holding three layers – top, wadding and backing fabric – together and at the same time adding a decorative effect. Most of the quilted projects in this book, such as the children's sleeping bags, can be worked either by hand or machine.

There are many different types of quilting and traditionally quilts were bedcovers. Now any number of fashion items and accessories around the home can be quilted for a decorative and practical effect. The shapes of the stitching can be grid-like or based on a motif design such as a leaf, flower, feather, heart or scallop.

Quilting and a patchwork effect are combined in this warm, stylish quilt. The large, bold quilting stitches and the tufts are part of the design, making this a quick-and-easy project to withstand the rigours of a child's handling.

Fabrics for quilting

Natural fabrics such as cotton and linen are ideal for quilting, particularly if you are working on a machine, because they do not slip and slide while you are stitching. The fabric used for the backing should be a similar weight and be easily pierced by a needle if you are working by hand. Calico is a good choice for this.

Fabrics with a sheen such as glazed cottons, silk and satin provide a dramatic effect because the reflected light adds interest to the quilting stitches and the overall pattern. Light-coloured fabrics set off quilted patterns better than dark ones.

Quilting can also look very attractive worked on more unusual surfaces such as soft leathers and suedes.

You should wash and iron the top and backing fabrics first to check for colour fastness and shrinkage. This also removes any dressing in the fabric so it will be softer and easier to handle.

Wadding for quilting

The wadding should be chosen according to the project. Bedcovers, which need warmth and bulk, should be filled with medium- or heavy-weight synthetic wadding. This is washable and comes in narrow widths that can be butted against each other and joined with a herringbone stitch (page 92). This avoids a ridge that would show through on the surface of the quilted fabric.

For more decorative quilting, such as wall hangings and accessories, use fleecy cotton or wool, light-weight synthetic wadding or interlining such as bump and domett for the filling.

The thicker the wadding, the more pronounced the quilting stitches will be, and also the more difficult to sew. Because synthetic wadding is pressed flat by ironing , it is best not to use it for items that require pressing, although quilting stitches tend to reduce the need for ironing. Unfold wadding before use to revive its bounce.

Preparing to quilt

If you have never quilted before, make some small experimental samples first to see which method you prefer. The method will also depend on the pattern for your quilting stitches. Straight lines are simple to quilt by hand or machine, but curves are quite tricky on the machine and you may find it easier to quilt them by hand or avoid curves altogether if you are a beginner.

Transferring the design

All quilting stitches follow a pattern and this needs to be transferred to the top fabric before you start. Straight lines can be drawn directly onto the fabric using a ruler and dressmakers' pen or tailors' chalk. Pencils in a colour close to the fabric can also be used.

A useful technique for hand quilting straight lines is to place masking tape on the fabric and use the straight edge as a guide for the quilting stitches. When one row is completed, simply lift the tape and place it where you want the next line.

More complicated designs are usually drawn onto the fabric using dressmakers' carbon paper. This is available from good haberdashery stores. It is placed carbon side down onto the right side of the main fabric. The tracing paper with the design drawn on it is placed on top and pinned or taped in place. With a lead pencil or tracing wheel, trace around the outline to impress the design on the fabric.

Another method which is more time-consuming is to make pin holes all along the lines of the design and then rub tailors' chalk through the perforations to leave a dotted line on the fabric. The dots are then joined with dressmakers' pencil, or with water-soluble or air-erasable pens. You can make the tiny holes by either pricking the lines with a needle at regular intervals or machine stitching with an unthreaded needle.

A traditional method for transferring a design for hand quilting is to use a blunt-ended tapestry or rug needle to mark the pattern as you work. With the needle held at an angle, draw it around the outline of a template, making a slight indentation in the fabric.

Hand quilting equipment
Traditionally, hand quilting was worked with the three layers stretched out on a frame, but unless you already have a frame, it is generally better to buy a quilting hoop, which is cheaper and much less bulky, and suitable for smaller items. This is much like an embroidery hoop, only larger, and is either supported on its own stand or rested against the edge of the table, leaving both hands free for quilting.

Using a frame
If you decide to use a frame for quilting, especially for larger items such as bedcovers, the fabric should not be stretched as tightly as for embroidery. Make sure the grain of the top and bottom fabrics are straight across the frame.

To attach the layers, start with the backing fabric. Align the edge of the fabric with the webbing on one of the runners. Pin and then sew to hold in place. Attach the top edge of the backing fabric to the other runner and roll up until the runners are parallel and about 50cm (20in) apart. Assemble the frame with the stretchers and pegs.

Next lay the wadding over the backing fabric, aligning one edge with the runner nearest you and pin to hold. Let the rest of the wadding hang over the top runner.

Lay the top fabric over the wadding and align with the edges of the backing fabric and

wadding and pin through all three layers onto the webbing. Tack in place with running stitches.

Smooth the fabric and, using fine long pins, pin all three layers together within a few centimetres of the top runner.

To hold the fabric taut at the sides, you will need tape and pins. Starting by the top runner, pin one end of the tape to the fabric layers. Bring the tape around the stretcher and pin to the fabric about 8cm (3in) away from the previous position. Repeat until both sides are secured.

Now work the quilting starting with the area closest to you. When the framed area has been quilted, unpin the tape and the layers near to the top runner. Unroll some backing fabric and then roll up the completed quilting onto the bottom runner. Secure the tapes and layers as before.

Hand sewing
You can either use ordinary thread appropriate to the fabric or special quilting thread, which is heavier and stronger. It is useful to have a block of beeswax, available from haberdashers, through which you can run the threads to prevent them from twisting during sewing.

Use short fine needles – No. 8 or 9 betweens – and a thimble.

Before sewing, tack the layers together thoroughly. Tack from the centre out to the corners and to equally spaced points at the edges, then start again at the centre and tack in concentric

squares spaced about 15cm (6in) apart. To avoid ending up with a concentration of tacking knots at the centre of the work, take a thread long enough to run from corner to corner. Start at the centre, leaving a long tail of thread, and tack out to one corner; return to the centre and rethread the needle, then tack out to the opposite corner.

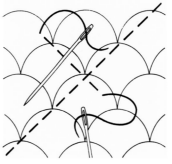

To position the work in a hoop, place the central part of the tacked work over the inside ring. Smooth over the outer edges and slide the outer ring in place. Then tighten the adjustment screw to hold the materials taut. After quilting, remove and reposition over the next section.

Quilt from the centre of the work outwards, holding the work in the hoop to keep the layers evenly stretched. Take a fairly short length of thread, about 40cm (16in) and knot one end. Lose the knot in between the top and bottom layers and quilt with a small, even running stitch. It helps to wear a thimble on the index finger of your sewing hand. Keep the other hand under the work to guide the needle back up again after it has passed through all three layers.

Quilting can also be worked in backstitch which gives a more defined line of stitching. This can form a decorative element in its own right, especially if worked in a contrasting colour or a slightly thicker thread.

Complete one section before moving on to the next, and never leave the work in a hoop overnight. To finish off a thread, tie a knot close to the last stitch and take the thread through to the back, losing the knot in the wadding. Run the needle along the wadding, bring it back up to the top and cut the end.

Machine quilting
When machine quilting, it is better to secure the layers with fine long pins rather than tacking threads which can get caught in the machine foot. Draw the design on the top fabric and then assemble the layers. Insert the pins parallel to the quilting lines or at right angles across them.

For machine quilting, use a slightly longer stitch than normal and loosen off the tension a little. Do not begin or end with a back stitch – the ends should be pulled through to the back, knotted in pairs and pulled up into the wadding with a needle.

Stitch from the centre to the edge, where possible, working out to one edge then returning to the centre and working out to the other edge. Hold the work flat with your hands, but avoid pushing the layers apart.

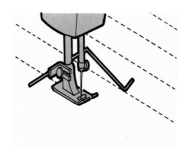

A quilting foot is a useful attachment which enables you to make evenly spaced lines of quilting, but it is not essential because you can always mark the lines on the fabric instead.

WHITE HANGING

Hunting through the piles in junk shops or at jumble sales, you will sometimes find old sheets or pillowcases, perhaps decorated with delicate embroideries, which are too beautiful to throw away but too worn for practical use. Here's a way to take the unworn sections and the pretty, embroidered motifs, and extract the maximum visual pleasure from them by turning them into a romantic but sophisticated wall hanging, a patchwork of antiques. If you have no monogrammed items, work your own embroideries, copying capitals from old books or prints.

Finished size: 114cm x 146cm (45in x 57½in)

MATERIALS

2.8m (3⅛yd) of 120cm (48in) wide fine, closely woven white cotton or linen, preferably old, but not too worn sheeting

1.5m (1¾yd) of 120cm (48in) wide white cotton fabric, for lining

2.2m (2½yd) of 100cm (39in) wide light-weight polyester wadding

Well-sharpened light-coloured pencil

Tracing paper

Dressmakers' carbon paper

Matching thread

METHOD

◻ From white cotton or linen fabric cut out twelve 35cm (14in) squares. Repeat with wadding and lining. Fold each square in half both ways and press to mark the centre point.

◻ For squares C, H, I and K mark the design straight on the fabric using a well-sharpened pencil in a light colour, following the diagrams on pages 90 and 91. Working from the centre point and using a ruler, mark out

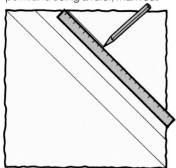

the pattern of straight lines for squares C, H and I. Use a clamshell template for the curved design in square K.

Mark from the centre out both ways till the square is complete.

◻ For squares A and F, it will be necessary to draw up the design first. Mark the correct size square on a sheet of paper and, using a compass and pencil, mark out each design. Transfer to the fabric: place the design centrally on the right side of the fabric and pin at each corner. Slide a sheet of

carbon paper, face downwards, between paper and fabric; trace out the design with a pencil or a tracing wheel.

◻ On all the quilting squares, place the top fabric with wrong side to lining, sandwiching the wadding in between. Adjust the sewing machine by loosening the tension and set the stitch length to a medium-size stitch. Quilt over the marked lines of each design in turn, using a quilting bar attachment to obtain evenly spaced lines of stitching. Begin by stitching the centre lines and then work outwards from the centre. Work all rows of stitching in the same direction to prevent puckering.

◻ For the embroidered squares: trace off the chosen initials, adding flowers and bows, as desired. Centre the tracing right side up on the fabric square and pin at each corner. Slide a piece of carbon paper face downwards between the tracing and the fabric. Mark over the design lines. Work each motif in padded satin stitch. Add a row of cross stitches as desired.

◻ When each embroidered square is complete, place a layer of wadding and then a layer of lining fabric and pin and tack together.

◻ To stitch the squares together, start by joining them into rows. Place squares with right sides together, then pin, tack and stitch through all layers. Trim wadding right back to stitching line to reduce bulk. Lightly press seams open. At each side of seam, turn top fabric and lining seam allowances in by 6mm (¼in) to meet each other and sew together with running stitch, by hand or machine. Lightly catchstitch seam allowances to lining to hold them flat.

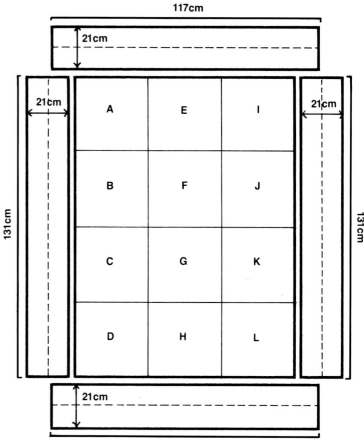

A

C

F

H

Machine quilting requires a certain degree of practice and skill and you may find that some of the quilting patterns shown here, especially those with curves, are too difficult for you. If so, you could either repeat some of the straight line patterns instead, or work quilting by hand. The squares would be easier to quilt in a hoop if you marked them out on a single piece of fabric, assembled the three layers of wadding, backing and top fabric together, and then cut the squares apart after quilting.

Squares **B, D, E, G, J** and **L** are unquilted and have embroidered initials, along the lines of the two examples given on the right.

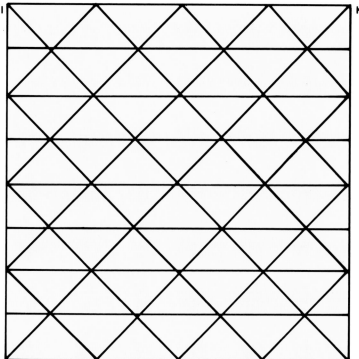

▦ When all rows are complete, join them together in the same manner as the squares.

▦ For the borders cut two strips for the side edges, each 131cm x 21cm (51in x 8¼in) and two strips for top and base edges, each 117cm x 21cm (46in x 8¼in). Pin, tack and stitch one edge of side strips to each side of hanging taking 1.5cm (⅝in) seam allowance.

Fold in half, turn under seam allowance and slipstitch remaining long edge to reverse side of hanging.

▦ Repeat, to bind the bottom edge in the same way, stitching across the side strips to form neat corners. Slipstitch up the side edges of borders. Bind the top edge in the same way, but leave the side edges open to form a casing for a hanging pole.

KAZAK QUILT

These felt picture symbols were taken from a book on the folk art of the Kazaks, a nomadic tribe of central Asia. This quilt, made from two layers of flannel with a thick layer of wadding in between, would be ideal for keeping at bay the sub-zero temperatures of a Kazak winter. The symbols are drawn with oriental precision and machined on to the top before the quilt is assembled and edged with black and green sheeting.

Finished size: 120cm × 156cm (48in × 60in)

MATERIALS

3.2m (3½yd) of 120cm (48in) wide grey flannel
50cm (⅝yd) of 178cm (70in) wide green sheeting
30cm (½yd) of 178cm (70in) wide black sheeting
2.4m (2¾yd) of 90cm (36in) wide heavy-weight wadding
Small amounts of red, turquoise, blue, prune, pink and yellow felt, for motifs
Suitable filling to pad motifs
Dressmakers' pattern paper
Matching threads

METHOD

▦ From grey flannel cut two pieces each 156cm × 100cm (60in × 39in).

▦ Draw up the motif designs from the diagram and, following the diagram for colours, carefully cut out from felts. Pin the motifs carefully on one flannel piece, as shown in the picture and diagram. Using matching thread, carefully tack each motif in place, sewing close to the edge and taking small stitches. Stuff a small amount of filling inside each motif as you stitch.

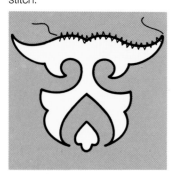

▦ Set the sewing machine to a close zigzag stitch – test on a spare piece of fabric before stitching. Zigzag stitch all round each motif. After stitching, take all the loose threads to the wrong side and tie in pairs.

▦ From green sheeting cut out one piece 160cm × 43cm (61½in × 17in). Taking a 1.5cm (⅝in) seam allowance and with right sides together, pin, tack and stitch one long edge of green sheeting to one long edge of front quilt piece, overlapping the flannel by 2cm (¾in) at either end. Repeat, to stitch remaining long edge of sheeting to one edge of quilt back in the same way. Fold the pieces together, forming a 20cm (8in) wide band of green sheeting at one edge.

▦ Cut two pieces of wadding each 120cm (48in) long. Butt the long edges against each other and join them together with herringbone stitch. Turn over and herringbone stitch on the other side to link them closely and securely. Trim wadding to measure 120cm × 156cm (48in × 60in).

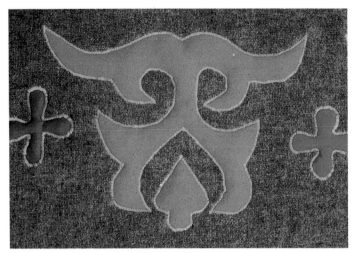

◨ Sandwich the wadding inside the quilt front and back; pin, and tack all the layers together. Fold the raw ends of the sheeting strip in to meet each other and cover the wadding. Slipstitch to close.

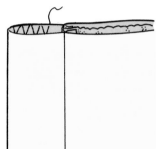

◨ Cut three strips of black sheeting: two 8cm × 101.5cm (3in × 40½in) and one 8cm × 160cm (3in × 61½in). Turn in the long edges on all strips by 1.5cm (⅝in) and press. Fold all strips down the centre and press.

◨ Take the two shorter strips and fold in 1.5cm (⅝in) at either short end and press, then position to cover raw ends on two short sides of quilt. Topstitch in place with white zigzag stitching. Where black strip meets green slipstitch in black to close.

◨ Apply final black strip in the same way, folding the raw ends into a mitre and slipstitching.

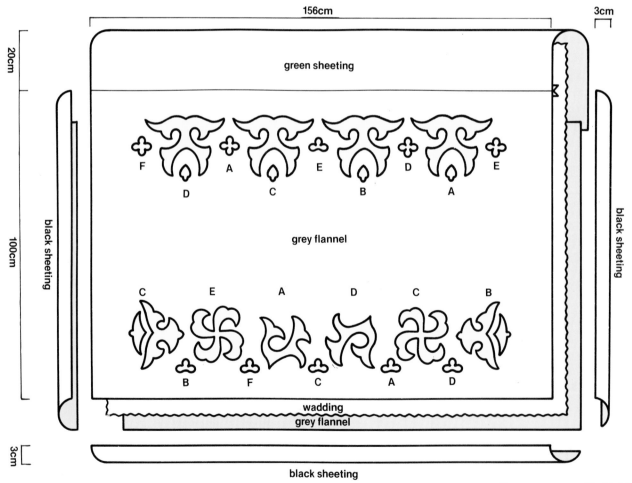

KEY

A *Red*
B *Prune*
C *Saffron yellow*
D *Pink*
E *Blue*
F *Turquoise*

Draw up your motifs (right); after cutting out from the chosen fabric, position on the quilt as shown above.

1 square = 5cm x 5cm (2in x 2in)

fold line

fold line

fold line

fold line

CONVERTIBLE BEDSPREAD

The perfect bedspread for a car enthusiast, and not all that difficult to make. The details are all topstitched to the main body, with a rolled-up sheet added as an optional extra, to make a seat back.

Finished size: approximately 270cm x 180cm (106in x 67in), to fit a 90cm (36in) wide bed – adjust the pattern for a narrower bed

MATERIALS

2.7m (3yd) of 178cm (70in) wide red sheeting
60cm (¾yd) of 90cm (36in) wide dark pink or red sheeting
1m (1yd) of 90cm (36in) wide grey cotton
2m (2⅛yd) of 90cm (36in) wide black cotton fabric
1.5m (1¾yd) of 90cm (36in) wide grey satin
80cm x 40cm (32in x 16in) of

striped cotton or fur fabric
40cm x 20cm (16in x 8in) of yellow cotton fabric
100cm (1⅛yd) of 100cm (39in) wide medium-weight polyester wadding
Buttons (for dashboard knobs)
1m (1⅛yd) of 2cm (¾in) wide woven black tape and buckles
Dressmakers' pattern paper
Matching threads

METHOD

▦ Draw up the patterns of the car from the diagram. From red sheeting, cut out outline, allowing a 1cm (⅜in) allowance all round. Turn the allowance to the wrong side; pin, tack and stitch in place, clipping into curves as necessary.

▦ Make up the car interior: position the grey fabric as shown in the diagram; pin, tack and zigzag stitch in place. Cut out two seats from striped fabric and two from wadding. Place wadding then fabric seats on the interior; pin, tack and zigzag stitch. Topstitch across seats, as shown.

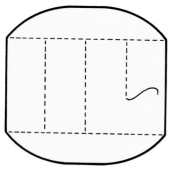

▦ From grey satin cut two door tops; pin, tack and zigzag stitch in place. Complete the interior with lines of stitching to form the dashboard, adding buttons.

▦ From black fabric, cut out two steering wheels, adding 1cm (⅜in) allowance all round. Cut one steering wheel from wadding, without seam allowance. Clipping into curves, turn under seam allowance round outside and inside of fabric wheels. Place steering wheels with wrong sides together, sandwiching wadding in between, and topstitch close to edge, making sure that no wadding is visible. Place in position on dashboard and fasten with stitching.

▦ From dark red or pink fabric, cut four wheel rims as shown in diagram, adding 1cm (⅜in) seam allowance. Turn under 6mm (¼in) double hem on two short straight edges of each piece. Neaten curved edges. Cut eight 40cm (16in) diameter wheels from black fabric. With

right sides facing, with 6mm (¼in) allowance, stitch wheels

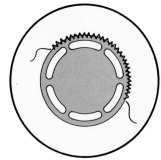

together in pairs, leaving a small opening in each pair. Turn to right side, press. Slipstitch opening.

▦ From grey satin cut out four hub caps. Apply to car wheels with zigzag stitching, adding centre detail. At each wheel position, pin and tack rims to fit behind wheel and edge of main car body. Topstitch all pieces.

▦ From grey satin cut out two headlights. Cut out two beams from yellow fabric. Place one on top of the other, with right sides up; pin, tack and zigzag stitch in place, adding highlights.

▦ From grey satin cut out bumpers, centre bonnet strip, rear lights, indicators, door sills and handles. Cut bumpers from wadding too. Place in position, with bumpers covering outer hemmed edge; pin, tack and zigzag stitch in place. Add number plates, embroidering with relevant name or number. Complete by zigzag stitching remaining design lines on body.

▦ For back straps, make up two 50cm (20in) long straps from tape. Add buckles to one end and cut the opposite end into a point. Position on bedspread, behind the interior, and stitch in place.

There is no need to follow these instructions implicitly; if your child identifies with a different style of car it will be an easy matter to change the position of the lights or alter the bonnet shape. Just move the main parts around till the car resembles one they recognize or just simply change the colour.

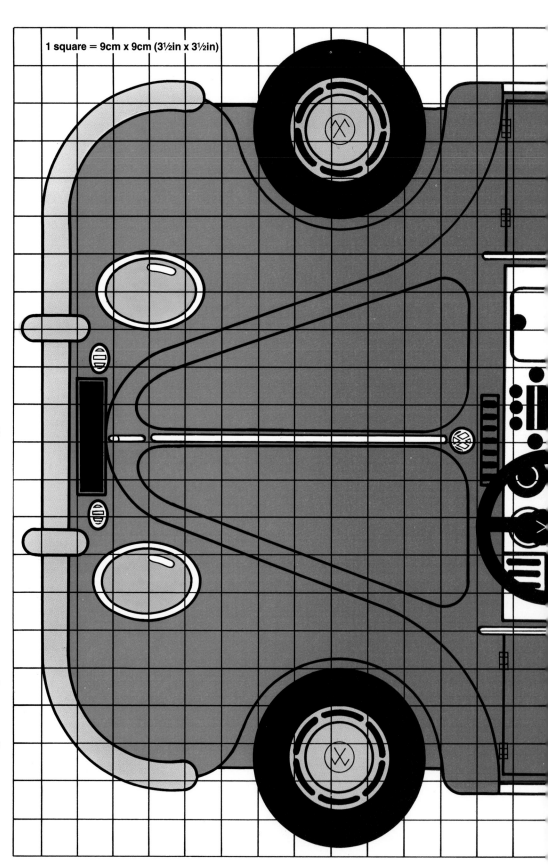

1 square = 9cm x 9cm (3½in x 3½in)

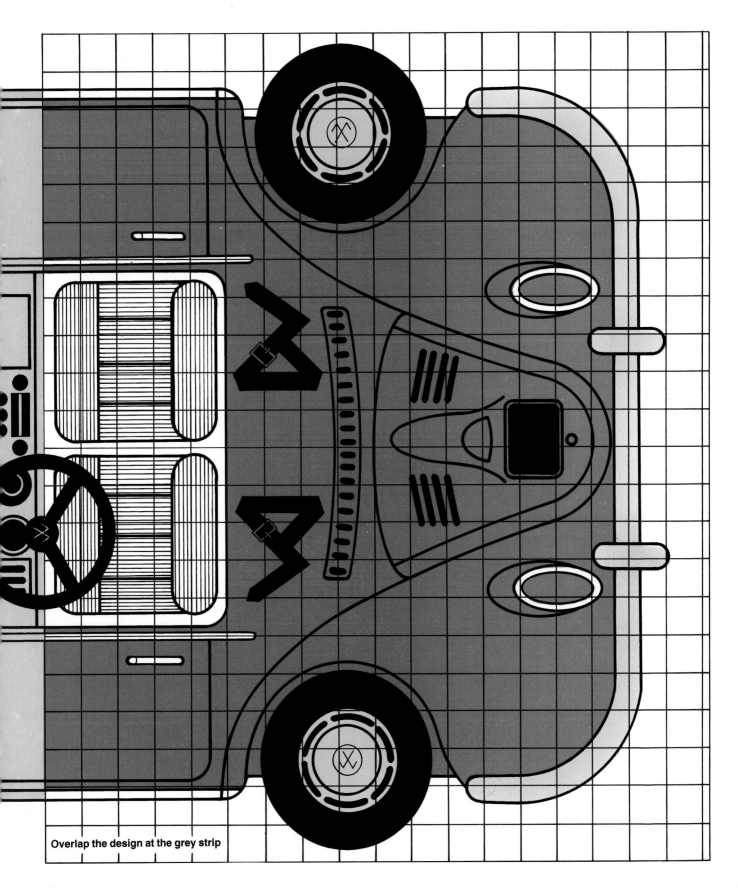

Overlap the design at the grey strip

CHILD'S COMFORTER

Turn a pattern of big, bold squares to your advantage by using it to provide the outlines for a quilt with the visual effect of patchwork. The quilting is worked by hand but with long, quick stitches which are meant to be noticed. The intersections are emphasized with tufts which also help to hold the wadding in place. The result is a cosy, stylish quilt – just the thing to keep a child warm (and asleep) on a cold night. But because it is so quick to make, it won't break your heart to see it jumped on, rolled up and sat on or subjected to the inevitable accidents of childhood.

Finished size: 144cm x 117cm (57in x 46½in), though the size can easily be adjusted to suit your needs or to fit in with the size of the pattern of your chosen fabric

MATERIALS

1.5m (1¾yd) of 120cm (48in) wide squared fabric

1.5m (1¾yd) of 120cm (48in) wide striped fabric

2.4m (2¾yd) of 90cm (36in) wide

heavy-weight wadding

Heavy cotton thread for quilting and knots

Matching threads

METHOD

▣ From squared fabric cut out one piece 147cm × 120cm (58¼in × 47¾in), which includes 1.5cm (⅝in) all round for seam allowance. Repeat, to cut a piece the same size from the striped fabric.

▣ Place the two fabric pieces with right sides together. Pin, tack and stitch together all round, leaving a 70cm (28in) central opening in one short side. Stitch round quilt again close to previous row of stitches. Trim and turn the 'bag' around to right side.

▣ Cut out two 117cm (46½in) lengths of wadding. Butt the long edges closely against each other and herringbone stitch along the join. Turn the wadding over and herringbone stitch over the join on the opposite side. Trim the width down to 144cm (57in) with the seam centrally placed. Insert the wadding inside the cover. Turn in the opening edges in line with the remainder of the seam and slipstitch together to close.

▣ Quilt the cover by hand along the squares of the design, as shown in the diagram, taking about 1.5cm (⅝in) per stitch. If your fabric has larger or smaller squares, you may have to adapt the quilting pattern slightly, but make sure that the lines are close enough to hold the layers.

▣ Make tufts of thread at each intersection: thread a needle with two or three lengths of heavy cotton thread. Push the needle through the quilt slightly to one side of the intersection and bring it up the same distance from the intersection on the opposite side. Tie the threads together over the intersection with a reef knot. Trim ends to 3cm (1¼in).

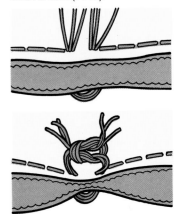

Make up the comforter from two different layers of fabric; pick one striped and one squared, so that you can flip it over on different days to change the look of the bed. Held inside by the handstitched quilting is a warm layer of wadding – follow the design lines of the fabric when stitching.

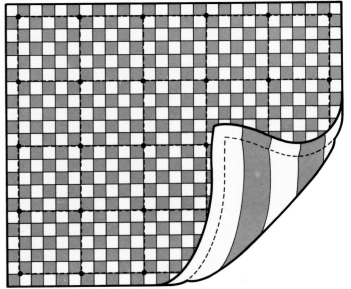

CRADLED IN COMFORT

Create a beautiful environment from which your baby can view the world with pleasure: whether you choose blue or pink, or play safe if you are a stickler for tradition, this pretty padded crib, complete with matching teddy, will be a wonderfully secure and cosy haven. The bag will prove invaluable for holding creams, cotton wool and other necessities, and if you have fabric – and energy – to spare you could make a tablecloth or even a nightdress to match. The crib will only last for a few months – an increasingly active baby will need something larger – but if the small scale and padded warmth help your baby to sleep soundly the effort will have been rewarded.

Sizes: crib approximately 120cm×60cm (47in×24in); bag 30cm×29cm (12in×11½in).

MATERIALS

FOR THE CRIB

4.4m (4⅞yd) of 228cm (90in) wide printed sheeting

4.4m (4⅞yd) of 90cm (36in) wide medium-weight wadding

1m (1yd) of 80cm (32in) wide buckram

4.2m (4¾yd) of 2.5cm (1in) wide ribbon

80cm x 35cm (32in x 14in) of 6mm (¼in) hardboard

79cm x 35cm (31in x 14in) cot mattress

25mm (1in) diameter dowel – four 1200mm (47in) lengths

50mm x 25mm (2in x 1in) planed beech – four lengths each 1200mm (47in) long, rounded off at the ends

2.6m (3yd) of 5cm (2in) wide upholstery webbing

Eight 50mm (2in) wood screws

Two 6cm (2½in) nuts and bolts, with washers

Glass paper

Matt varnish

FOR THE BAG

50cm (⅝yd) of 228cm (90in) wide printed fabric

60cm (¾yd) of 90cm (36in) wide plastic fabric

50cm (⅝yd) of 90cm (36in) wide lightweight wadding

Matching thread

FOR THE TEDDY

Oddments of printed fabric

Suitable filling

1m (1yd) of 1cm (⅜in) wide ribbon

Matching thread

METHOD

THE CRIB

▦ Smooth off the ends of the planed wood pieces with glass paper. Varnish, sanding down between each coat.

▦ Drill a hole 2.5cm (1in) down from one end (the top) and another hole 7.5cm (3in) up from the other end of each piece. Also drill a hole for the bolt, 5cm (2in) above the centre point of each piece, countersinking two of the pieces.

▦ Cross over the two pairs of end pieces, with the countersunk pieces on the outside, and fasten each pair with a nut and bolt, adding washers in between.

▦ Place dowel between crossed pieces, at the base of each piece, and screw in place. Repeat, to fit lengths of dowel at the top.

▦ Cut the webbing in half and join each piece to make two

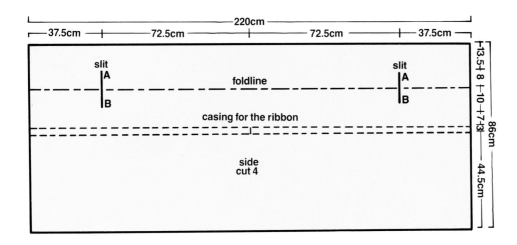

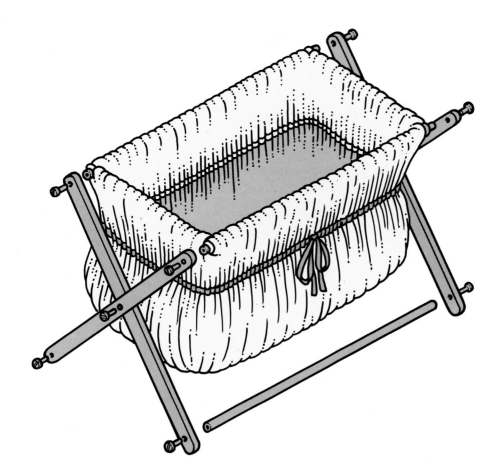

rings, each 122cm (48in) around, overlapping the ends and stitching very securely.

▦ Cut four pieces of sheeting each 220cm×86cm (87in×34in) for sides and two pieces each 83cm×38cm (32½in×15in) for base. Also cut two sides 217cm×83cm (85¾in×32¾in) from wadding and one base from buckram.

▦ Place the sides in pairs with right sides together and edges matching and join to make two rings. Lay the wadding pieces flat, meeting end to end, and join with herringbone stitch down one short end. Turn over and herringbone stitch the other side, then join the other short ends in the same way, so that there are no bulky seams.

▦ Sandwich wadding between the two fabric rings, right sides of fabric facing outwards. At the top, turn the fabric seam allowances in to meet each other, enclosing the wadding, and either slipstitch or machine topstitch together.

▦ Pin and tack the three layers of the side piece thoroughly, then machine quilt lengthwise down the fabric in straight lines, spaced 5cm (2in) apart. With the fabric facing outwards and buckram sandwiched in the middle, stitch the base layers together around the outside, taking a 1.5cm (⅝in) seam allowance. Trim buckram right back to seamline. Quilt the layers together as for the sides.

▦ Cut four 20cm (8in) slits in side where marked on pattern. Bind each slit in same way: cut two strips of fabric each 20cm by 10cm (8in by 4in). Fold each strip in half lengthwise, wrong sides together. Place a folded strip on either side of slit with raw edges facing inwards. On one side stitch the complete

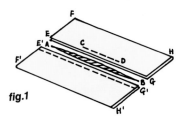

fig.1

length of the slit. On opposite side just stitch the central 10cm (4in) C to D *(fig. 1)*. Turn strips through to wrong side *(fig.2)*. Tack E′-F′ to A-C *(fig.3)*. Fold short end of second strip onto first strip matching E-C to E′-F′ Stitch E-C to E′-F′ then E-F to E′-C′ *(fig.4)*. Repeat for G-H etc. This binds slit *(fig.5)*.

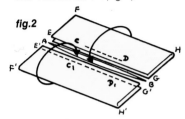

fig.2

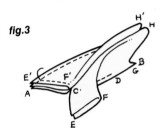

fig.3

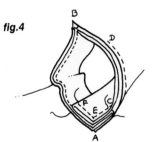

fig.4

fig.5

▦ Work a 2cm (¾in) vertical buttonhole in the centre of one side, 44.5cm (17½in) up from the base edge, as shown.

▦ Turn over the top edge along the foldline and pin and tack in position. Topstitch two rows of stitching, as shown, 3cm (1¼in) apart to form a casing.

▦ Work two rows of gathering stitches round the base edge of sides. Pull up gathers evenly to fit base. Join sides to base, gently rounding off the corners. Fold in

raw edges of fabric to meet each other and topstitch along fold to neaten.

▦ Thread ribbon round top casing and pull up till the top measures 300cm (118½in). Tie in a knot and then a bow.

▦ Push a webbing ring through either short end, bringing the ends of the ring through the openings. Unscrew the top dowel pieces of the cot and insert through the casing and through the ends of the webbing rings, then rescrew them in position.

▦ Place hardboard in cot to shape the base, then place mattress on top.

THE BAG

▦ From printed fabric cut out two pieces each 33cm×32cm (13in×12½in) for back and front, one piece 92cm×10.5cm (37in×4¼in) for the gusset. Repeat to cut out the same pieces from plastic. Also from plastic cut two pockets 32cm×17cm (12in×6¾in). From printed fabric cut two pieces for handles 42cm×8cm (16½in×3¼in). Cut out two pieces from wadding each 30cm×29cm (11¾in×11¼in) and one piece 89cm×7.5cm (35¾in×3in).

▦ Centre the wadding pieces over the relevant fabric pieces, placing wadding on the wrong side of the fabric and leaving a fabric margin of 1.5cm (⅝in) all around. Pin and tack together, tacking each way across the centre first and then at intervals of about 10cm (4in). Using a machine straight stitch or a hand running stitch, quilt diagonally across the fabric both ways to quilt back, front and gusset in a diamond pattern, with the lines spaced 4cm (1½in) apart.

▦ Turn down the top edge of one pocket to form a double 1cm (⅜in) hem. Pin, tack and stitch hem. Repeat for second pocket.

▦ With wrong side of pocket to right side of plastic front and matching base edges and sides (to height of pocket sides), pin, tack and stitch pocket to plastic front. Repeat to stitch other pocket to plastic back.

▦ Take strips for handles and fold each in half lengthwise with right sides together. Pin, tack and stitch raw edges, leaving an opening centrally in one side. Trim and turn to right side. Turn in opening edges in line with the remainder of the seam and slipstitch together to close. Topstitch all around each handle

close to the edges.

▦ Place one handle on back and one on front fabric sections of bag: the handles should lie on the surface of the front or back, 7.5cm (3in) in from either side and with the raw ends of the handles projecting 2.5cm (1in) beyond the raw top edge of the fabric. Tack in place at fabric seamline.

▦ With right sides together, place plastic front over fabric front, enclosing handle, and stitch along top seamline, taking a 1.5cm (⅝in) seam allowance. Turn right side out, bringing up handle, and topstitch 2cm (¾in) below top edge. Tack plastic and fabric together along side and base. Repeat for bag back.

▦ With right sides together and taking a 1.5cm (⅝in) seam, stitch fabric and plastic gusset pieces together across the short ends. Turn right side out.

▦ Matching short edges of gusset to top edge of front, stitch front to gusset, taking a 1.5cm (⅝in) seam. Repeat to stitch back to gusset. Trim seam allowances back to a scant 6mm (¼in).

▦ Pinching gusset and front or back together, topstitch around seams joining bag to gusset, enclosing the raw edges on the inside of the bag.

THE TEDDY

▦ Draw up the pattern to the desired size and cut two pattern pieces from fabric.

▦ Place the two pieces with right sides together and pin, tack and stitch together all around, leaving an opening in one side. Stitch again, close to previous line of stitching. Trim and turn to right side.

▦ Fill the teddy firmly. Turn in opening edges in line with the remainder of the seam. Slipstitch to close.

▦ Tie a ribbon around teddy's neck, forming it into a bow.

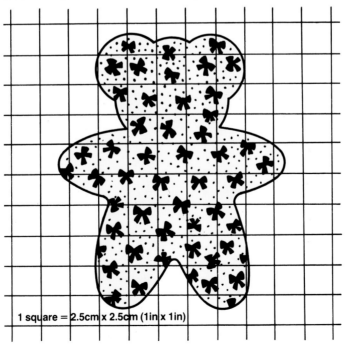

1 square = 2.5cm x 2.5cm (1in x 1in)

SLEEPING CAT AND DOG

Getting children to go to bed can be quite a problem, especially in long summer-holiday evenings, but you'll find it a whole lot easier with the help of these cheerful sleeping bags. Although they may look as if they entail a lot of work, they are in fact relatively quick and simple to make. Choose suitably doggy or catlike material, with a striped or spotted pattern, and – most important of all – washable.

MATERIALS

For either bag:
7m (7⅔yd) of 90cm (36in) wide striped or spotted cotton fabric
3.5m (4yd) of 90cm (36in) wide muslin
100cm (39in) wide heavy-weight polyester wadding, 200g (8oz):

4m (4½yd) for the cat or 3.5m (4yd) for the dog
50cm (20in) square of plain black cotton fabric (dog only)
Dressmakers' pattern paper
Dressmakers' carbon paper
Embroidery cottons
Matching threads

METHOD

FOR EITHER ANIMAL

▦ Draw up pattern from diagram and cut out from stated fabrics, adding a 1.5cm (⅝in) seam allowance round each fabric piece and wadding pieces for main body and for the head pieces.

▦ Make up the fore and hind legs in the same way: place the two pieces of each limb with right sides together, raw edges matching; pin, tack and stitch all round, leaving the edge that will join to body open. Trim and turn to right side. Insert wadding; pin, tack and stitch across open edges. Topstitch each limb as indicated.

▦ For the tail, cut a strip of fabric 70cm (28in) long and 20cm (8in) wide and, folded right sides together, join across one end and down long side. Cut strip of wadding to match, roll it up and unfold tail, right side out, over wadding. Pin, tack and stitch across top end.

▦ Place one body front to muslin, sandwiching wadding in between. Pin, tack and topstitch across body, following stripes (on cat) or rows of spots (dog) as a guide. Stop short at the seamline, 1.5cm (⅝in) in from the raw edges. Repeat for back body.

▦ For each body piece, stitch

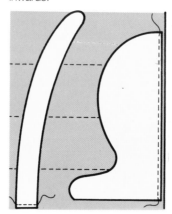

through all three layers along seamline right round the edge, then trim back edge of wadding close to seamline. Lay the legs and tail on top of front body, matching edges at the points where limbs join body. Pin, tack and stitch in position, still lying inwards.

▦ Pin back body to front, right sides facing, leaving top edge free. Tack and then stitch all round, catching in legs and tail.

▦ Dog's ears: place each pair of ear pieces right sides together. Pin, tack and stitch round outer edge, leaving joining edge open. Turn right side out, insert wadding, then topstitch by hand to hold wadding in place, stitching close to outer edge all round. Pin, tack and stitch straight across open edge.

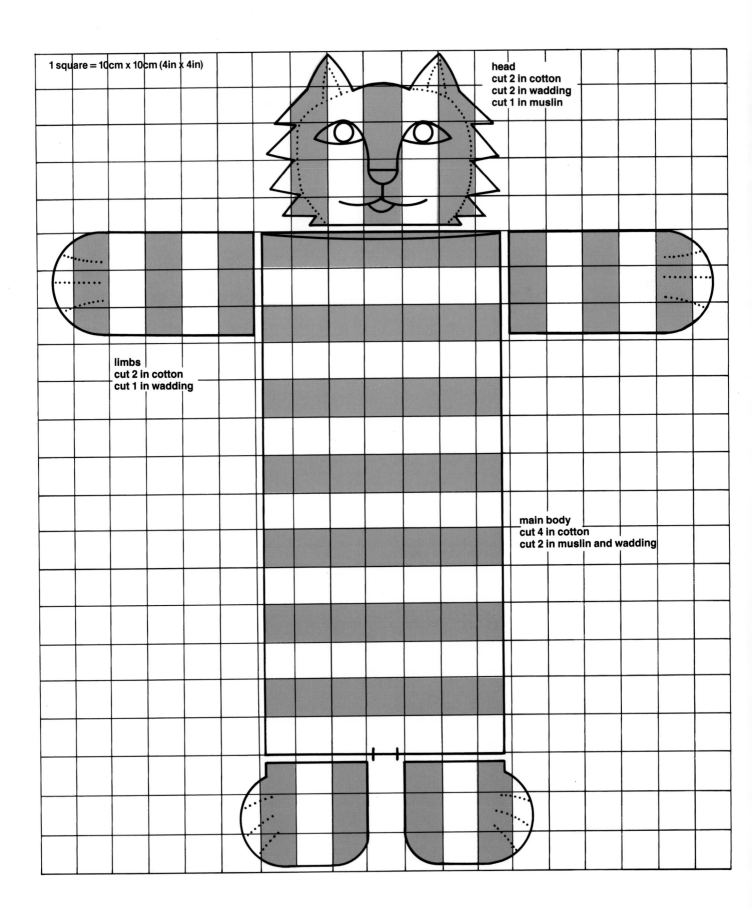

1 square = 10cm x 10cm (4in x 4in)

head
cut 2 in cotton
cut 2 in wadding
cut 1 in muslin

limbs
cut 2 in cotton
cut 1 in wadding

main body
cut 4 in cotton
cut 2 in muslin and wadding

▦ Using carbon paper, lightly mark in features on one head piece. Place on a layer of wadding backed by a layer of muslin. Embroider features in straight stitch, either by hand or machine.

▦ For dog, lay ears on front head, lying inwards and matching joining edges.

▦ For either bag, place back head with right sides to front head; pin, tack and stitch together, leaving neck edge free. Trim wadding from seam allowance and turn head right side out. Insert second layer of wadding, then pin, tack and stitch straight across neck edge.

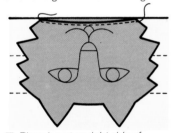

▦ Place head on right side of back body, matching neck edge with centre of top edge of body. Pin and tack in place.

▦ Make up the bag lining from two remaining body pieces: place with right sides together; pin, tack and stitch all round, leaving top edge open and a central opening in base edge. Place lining over sleeping bag with right sides together, top edges matching. Pin, tack and stitch all round top edge, catching in head.

▦ Pull up lining and turn in opening edge, in line with remainder of seam; pin, tack and stitch to close. Push lining down inside bag.

▦ If desired, add a fabric tie to the end of the tail and a button to the base, so the bag can be rolled up and tied.

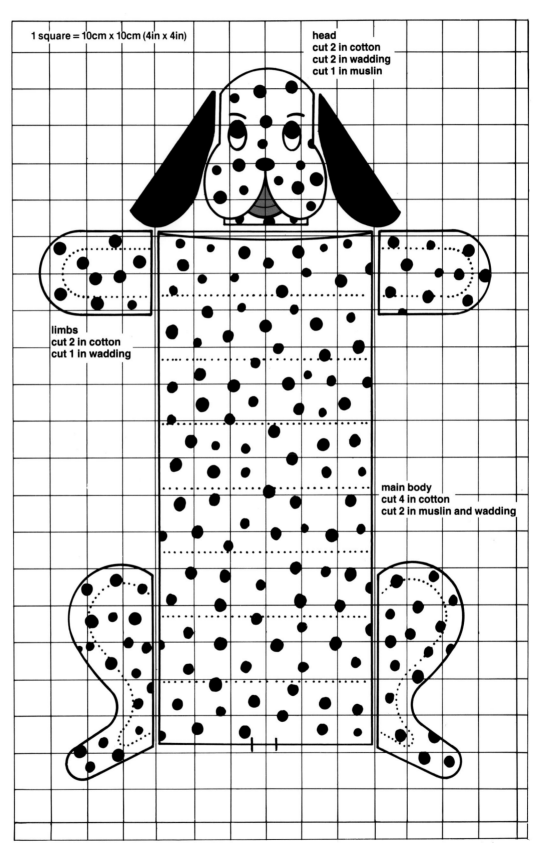

1 square = 10cm x 10cm (4in x 4in)

head
cut 2 in cotton
cut 2 in wadding
cut 1 in muslin

limbs
cut 2 in cotton
cut 1 in wadding

main body
cut 4 in cotton
cut 2 in muslin and wadding

MIDNIGHT MONSTERS

Your children will love these friendly prehistoric sleeping bags, and they'll probably be able to tell you the names of the dinosaurs without looking them up. Just to remind you they are: dimetrodon (green), protoceratops (blue) and triceratops (maroon). Although they look impressively complicated, they are not all that difficult to make, especially as the quilting, which can be worked by hand or machine, is intended to produce an authentically wrinkled-looking surface. The edges are also easy to finish, as they are covered with bias binding.

MATERIALS

FOR EACH BAG
2.2m (2¼yd) of 115cm (45in) wide cotton for back, in colour of your choice
3.8m (4¼yd) of 100cm (39in) wide heavy-weight polyester wadding (if your machine cannot take heavy-weight wadding, use the medium weight)
Fusible webbing
Quilting threads
Dressmakers' pattern paper
Matching threads

In addition you will need:

DIMETRODON
6m (6½yd) of 115cm (45in) wide percale or glazed cotton in green
50cm (⅝yd) as above in navy
6.6m (7¼yd) of 2cm (¾in) wide bias binding in green and 1.5m (1⅝yd) in navy
Oddment of pale yellow cotton fabric

PROTOCERATOPS
4.5m (5yd) of 115cm (45in) wide percale or glazed cotton in navy
1.6m (1⅓yd) as above in bright blue
4.6m (5yd) of 2cm (¾in) wide bias binding in bright blue and 2.5m (2¾yd) in navy
Oddments of pale yellow and pink cotton fabrics

TRICERATOPS
5.8m (6½yd) of 115cm (45in) wide maroon percale or glazed cotton
7.6m (8½yd) of 2cm (¾in) wide maroon bias binding
Oddment of pale yellow fabric

METHOD

DIMETRODON
▦ Scale up the pattern on to dressmakers' pattern paper and cut one complete outline in cotton and one in green percale or glazed cotton. They must make a matching pair (with wrong sides together). If you are making two bags and want the heads of finished bags to face each other when your children are using them, bear this in mind when cutting. Also cut one whole outline from wadding.
▦ Cut along neckline of pattern and cut out one whole body only from percale and one from wadding (the percale should lie wrong side up in same direction as previous pieces).
▦ Cut along lines between upper and lower body and tail. Cut out body top in green percale. Adding 1cm (⅜in) along top edge but not along outer edge, cut belly and tail from navy percale.

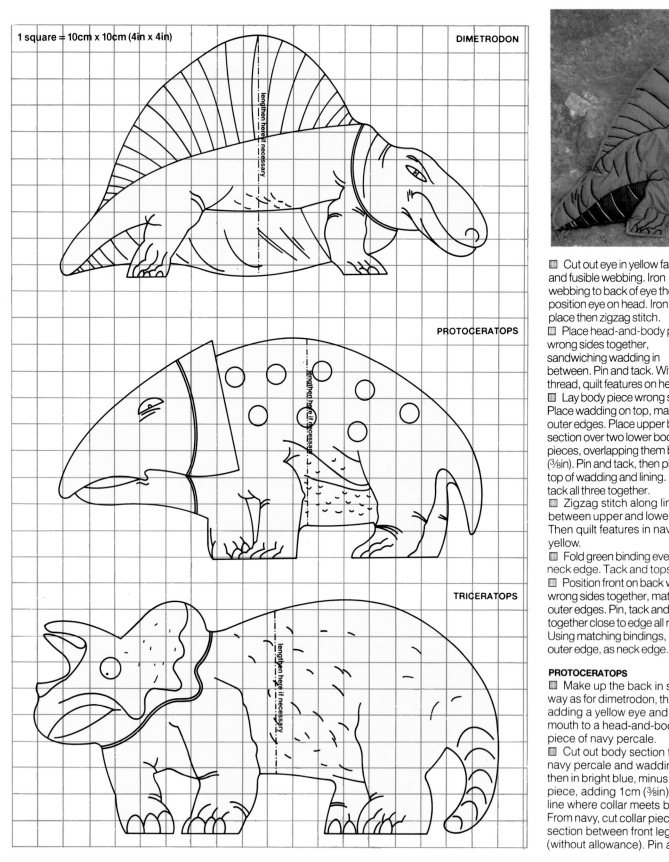

1 square = 10cm x 10cm (4in x 4in)

DIMETRODON

lengthen here if necessary

PROTOCERATOPS

lengthen here if necessary

TRICERATOPS

lengthen here if necessary

▦ Cut out eye in yellow fabric and fusible webbing. Iron webbing to back of eye then position eye on head. Iron in place then zigzag stitch.
▦ Place head-and-body pieces wrong sides together, sandwiching wadding in between. Pin and tack. With navy thread, quilt features on head.
▦ Lay body piece wrong side up. Place wadding on top, matching outer edges. Place upper body section over two lower body pieces, overlapping them by 1cm (⅜in). Pin and tack, then place on top of wadding and lining. Pin and tack all three together.
▦ Zigzag stitch along line between upper and lower body. Then quilt features in navy and yellow.
▦ Fold green binding evenly over neck edge. Tack and topstitch.
▦ Position front on back with wrong sides together, matching outer edges. Pin, tack and stitch together close to edge all round. Using matching bindings, bind outer edge, as neck edge.

PROTOCERATOPS
▦ Make up the back in same way as for dimetrodon, this time adding a yellow eye and pink mouth to a head-and-body piece of navy percale.
▦ Cut out body section from navy percale and wadding, then in bright blue, minus collar piece, adding 1cm (⅜in) along line where collar meets body. From navy, cut collar piece and section between front legs (without allowance). Pin and

112

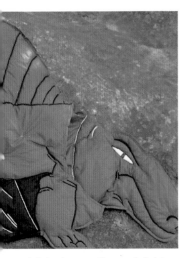

tack inter-leg section on bright blue body, overlap and tack collar to body.

▦ From fusible webbing cut out eight 6cm (2½in) diameter spots. Place on wrong side of navy fabric and iron in place. Cut out spots, place on front body and iron in place.

▦ Put the three layers of body section together. Zigzag stitch around spots, neckline and inter-leg section and quilt features, then bind neck and outer edges as for dimetrodon.

TRICERATOPS
▦ This is made up in the same way as the two previous animals.
▦ If the bag needs to be wider, fill in the spaces between the legs with grass green or sand fabric to produce a straight edge down that side and continue the **opening down the front leg.**

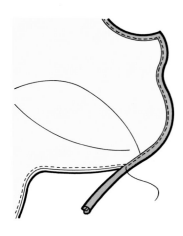

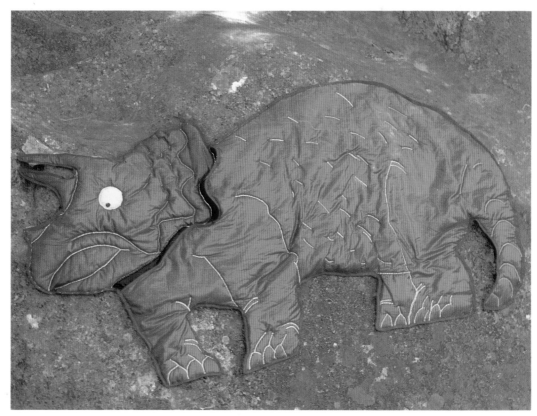

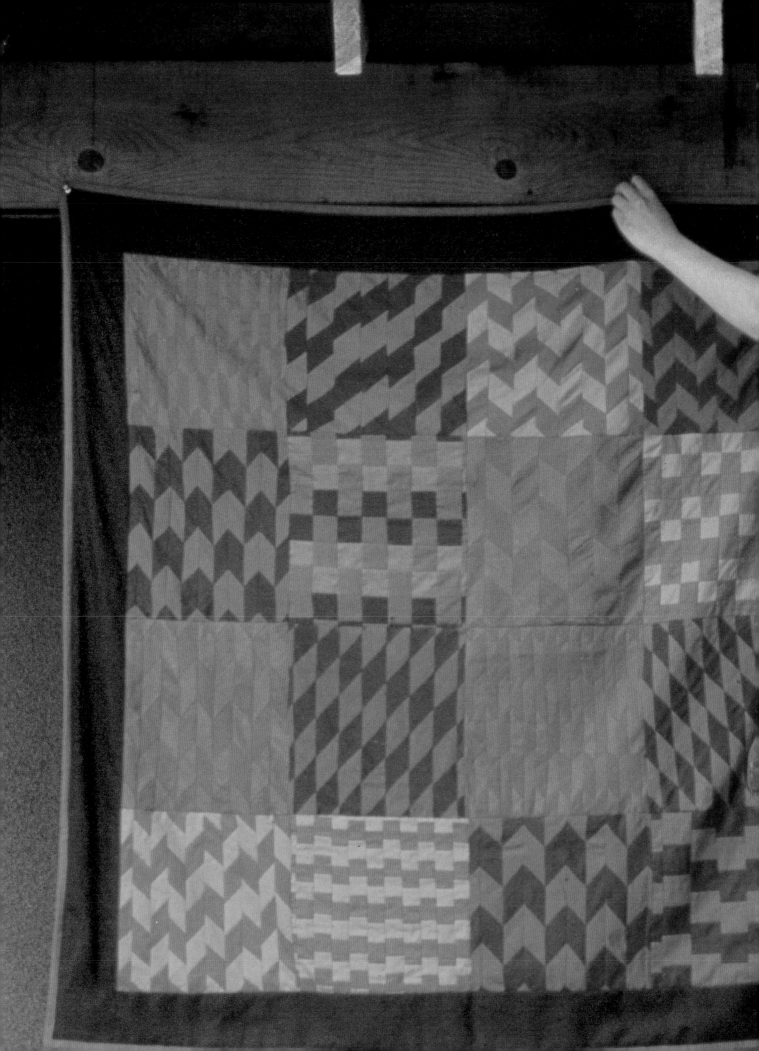

PATCHWORK

BASIC ESSENTIALS

The sewing skills used for patchwork are the same as those needed for dressmaking and the key to success is in the planning of the design and the use of colour and pattern.

Traditional patchwork is when pieces of cloth are stitched together to create a whole new fabric. The fabric is cut using templates of geometric shapes such as diamonds, triangles, squares and hexagons, and these pieces are then sewn together by hand or machine. Another method is crazy patchwork where irregular shapes and embroidery stitches are combined to create a brilliant effect.

Patchwork has close links with appliqué. The simplest way to achieve a patchwork effect is to appliqué ribbon strips onto backing fabric.

This patchwork wall hanging is made up of blocks of different patterns based on triangles. Calico and shades of denim combine to make a simple but effective colour scheme.

Colour variations

There is no reason why the colours suggested for the patchwork designs should not be changed to suit your personal preference, and in fact it is not always possible to find the same colours as shades go in and out of fashion.

Sometimes, however, a change of colour can alter the appearance of a design, particularly in the case of patchwork, which depends for its effect on a good contrast of colours and light and dark tones. If you are thinking of using a different selection of colours, the best way to check that your idea will work is to make a small-scale copy of the design on graph or isometric paper, with no colours filled in; take several tracings, and then experiment with a succession of different colour variations, using felt tipped pens or crayons.

Another method, which is particularly useful if you are not sure whether a blend of patterned fabrics will work well together, is to make a small-scale outline of the design and then cut fabric patches, to this scale and without seam allowances. Stick them down on the paper and you will have at least a fairly good idea of how well they will work together when the patches are scaled up to the full size.

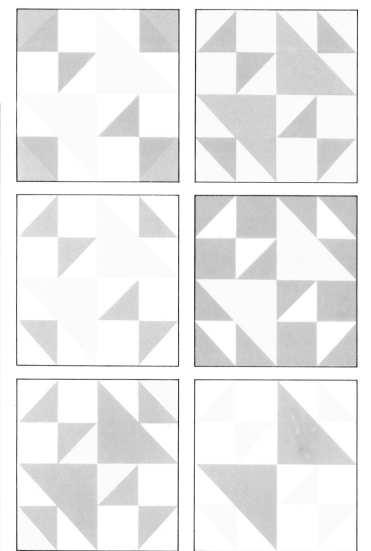

Choosing fabrics

The easiest fabric to use for patchwork is pure dress-weight cotton, but you can also use silks or wools. Avoid mixing fabrics of different weights and types as they will tend to pull unevenly against each other. You can mix textures as long as the fabrics are similar in weight. The exception is the type of patchwork which is applied to a background fabric like the Crazy Cover (p118), where it is perfectly possible to mix weights and textures. Make sure that you have enough fabric to complete your design.

Making templates

The simplest way is to draw each shape to the full size on graph paper, stick the paper to card and then cut it out with a craft knife.

For hand sewing, make templates to the full size minus seam allowances. For machine sewing, make templates to include seam allowances.

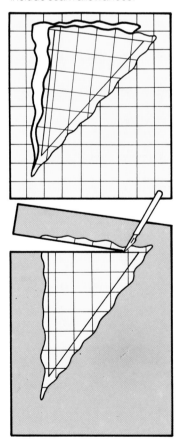

Marking and cutting

For hand-sewn work, start by drawing a guideline on the wrong side of the fabric, parallel to the selvedge and at least a seam allowance away from it. Place the template against this line, starting at one corner of the piece, and draw round it. Add a seam allowance. Position the template on the line again, a seam allowance away from the outer marked line (cutting edge of first patch), and repeat. As you work, try to butt the patches up against each other as much as possible to save fabric.

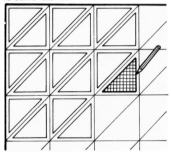

Cut the patches out along the outer marked line – the inner line is the sewing line – and sort them into piles according to shape and colour.

For machine patchwork, you only need the cutting edge to be marked, since the edge of the presser foot or a piece of masking tape stuck to the base plate can be used as a guide to the seamline.

For both hand and machine work, try to mark out patches so that as many edges as possible are in alignment with the grain lines of the fabric.

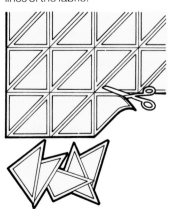

Hand sewing

Pin two patches with right sides together, putting a pin at each corner first and then at intervals along the sewing line. Insert the pins at right angles to the sewing line. Take a length of thread about 35cm (14in) long and thread your needle. Make a knot in the other end, which should be the end you have just cut. Using a small, neat running stitch, sew the patches together, sewing along the marked seamline only, not in the seam allowance. Finish with two or three back stitches and press the seam to one side. Join patches into rows and then rows into larger sections, always pressing seams to one side.

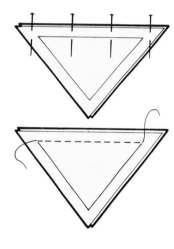

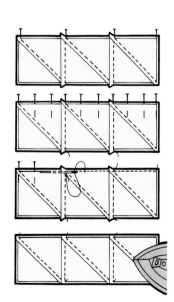

Machine sewing

Pin patches together, pinning across the unmarked seamline. Set your machine to 5 stitches per centimetre (about 12 per inch) and stitch patches together, removing pins before they pass under the presser

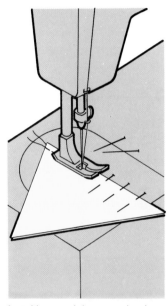

foot. You can join several pairs of patches together at one sitting, leaving a short length of thread between each pair. When you have finished, separate the pairs and press all seams before joining the patches into larger units.

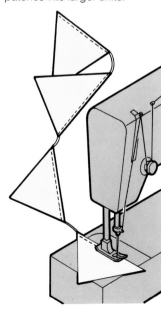

CRAZY COVER

If you enjoy going to extremes when it comes to lavishly embellished and ornate surroundings, make yourself a richly patterned and textured cover along the lines of this antique crazy quilt. The Victorians called this type of work crazy patchwork because the patches are completely random and can be decorated with anything that comes to hand – signatures, sentimental mementoes, ribbons, buttons and, of course, embroidery stitches. So raid your wardrobe, cut up all your outdated evening dresses and start sewing!

MATERIALS

Assortment of scraps or remnants of various fabrics – silks, velvets, brocades or cottons
Background fabric in light-weight calico or cotton, sufficient for the desired size of cover
Backing fabric of cotton to line the finished patchwork
Embroidery cottons in different colours
Matching threads

METHOD

▦ The patchwork can either be sewn as one piece or, to make it easier to handle, in squares or rectangles of manageable size which can be joined together when the work is complete.

▦ Start by cutting patches and dividing them into colours and shades so that you can make sure that you have a good blend as you progress. Remember that they will be much smaller once you have overlapped them and turned under raw edges. Avoid sharp points or tight curves.

▦ If some of the patches which you wish to use are rather small, join them together to make more usable strips.

▦ If you are making the cover in sections, cut the background fabric into squares or rectangles, making sure that they are all the same size.

▦ Whether you are working the whole cover or sections, begin by positioning a right-angled patch on one corner of the background fabric and pinning. Work across from this point, adding further patches to cover the raw edges of the previous ones and overlapping by at least 1cm (⅜in). It helps to work on a large flat surface and to leave all patches

but the first unpinned until you are happy that you have a really attractive combination of colours and tones.

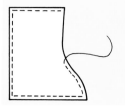

▦ Use your pieces of strip patchwork to cover long raw edges and provide a contrast in size.

▦ When the backing fabric is covered and you have checked that no small areas of it are showing through, pin all the patches in position.

▦ There are several ways of sewing the patches in position. The quickest method is to tack down the patches without turning the edges under and then sew them with a machine zigzag stitch, covering raw edges.

▦ The more traditional method, and the one which you should use if you intend to combine the patchwork with hand embroidery stitches, as on the example shown here, is to turn under and tack overlapping edges and then sew them with either a small

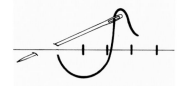

running stitch or a blind stitch. If the embroidery stitch is dense enough, then you can simply embroider the patches in position. If not, embroider after the patches have been handsewn or machine stitched on to the backing fabric.

▦ Leave raw edges at the outer edge of the work. If you are working in sections, trim completed sections to the same size then join them with a 1cm (⅜in) seam, sewing through all layers. Press seams open.

▦ Cut and join strips of the backing fabric to make a piece large enough to back the cover. Either cut the backing to the same size as the work, sew round the edge with right sides together and leaving an opening, turn right side out and slipstitch to close, or make a self binding. To do this, cut the backing 6.5cm (2½in) larger than the patchwork all round. With wrong sides together, lay the top over the backing. Turn under raw edge of backing by 1.5cm (⅝in) then bring it over raw edge of top, folding in a mitre at the corners, and topstitch in position.

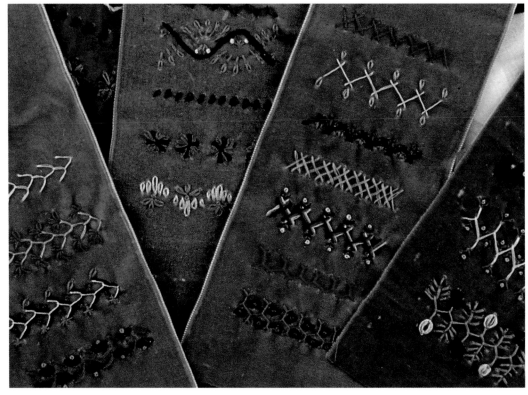

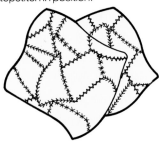

If you don't have the time to make a full-scale cover like the one shown here, why not make something smaller and more manageable, at least to start with? The Victorians used crazy quilting for various small objects such as cushions and tea cosies, firescreens or small tablecloths.

1 Basic cross stitch

2 Basic feather stitch

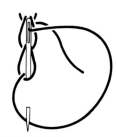

3 Basic chainstitch

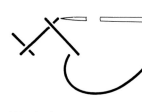

4 Herringbone

5 Open Cretan stitch

6 Feathered chainstitch

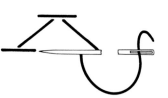

7 Chevron stitch

8 Closed buttonhole stitch

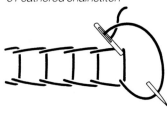

9 Square chainstitch

INDIAN MAGIC

Traditional patchwork techniques are here combined with richly patterned paisley prints, a type of fabric design which originated in India. The result is a collection of cushions and covers which create a warm and luxurious ambience, and which would bring a touch of Indian summer to a cold, north-facing room even in the depths of winter. The patches are all sewn on to a foundation square as they are joined together, making the finished pieces practical and hardwearing as well as attractive to look at.

MATERIALS

ALL COVERS AND CUSHIONS
Assorted patchwork fabrics –
plain and patterned fabrics,
either cottons or silks
Foundation fabric – a firm cotton

would be ideal
Coloured pencils
Matching threads

In addition you will need:

BED SQUARE
Ribbons for patchwork

LOG CABIN TABLECLOTH
3m (3¼yd) of 90cm (36in) wide
fabric for backing
1.5m (1⅝yd) of suitable fabric for
border

25cm (10in) square of red fabric
Long ruler

OBLONG CUSHION
60cm (¾yd) of 90cm (36in)
wide fabric for cushion back
33cm (13in) zip
2.4m (2¾yd) edging cord

Ribbons for patchwork
4 tassels
60cm x 50cm (24in x 20in)
cushion pad

OCTAGONAL CUSHION
Ribbons for patchwork
60cm (¾yd) of 90cm (36in) wide
fabric for cushion back
30cm (12in) zip

1.2m (1⅓yd) of 90cm (36in) wide
plain cotton fabric for cushion
pad
Suitable filling

METHOD

THE BED SQUARE

▦ Cut out and make up (if necessary) a foundation square measuring 160cm (63in). Mark the centre of the square with tacking stitches from corner to corner.

▦ For the centre, cut out one 35cm (13¾in) square (1), adding 6mm (¼in) seam allowance all round. Place right side up at centre of foundation square, as shown. Pin and stitch in place.

▦ Cut four isosceles triangles (2) with two sides 25cm (10in) long and one side 35cm (13¾in), adding seam allowance all round.

Place each triangle wrong side up on square, one by one, matching long edges, pinning and stitching and then turning the triangle over to lie right side up.

▦ Cut four isosceles triangles (3) with two sides 35cm (13¾in) and one side 50cm (20in), plus seam allowances, and apply in the same way.

▦ Cut two strips (4) to the length of the patchwork and 8cm (3in) wide and apply to two facing sides of the patchwork square. Cut two strips (5) the same width and the length of patchwork plus border strips. Apply to remaining sides.

◫ Cut four isosceles triangles (6) with two sides of 77cm (31in), divided by a right angle. Apply to patchwork as shown.

◫ Cut four border strips (7) measuring 160cm x 10cm (63in x4in). Attach the top and bottom strips along the inside edge, stopping 9.5cm (3¾in) short of the edge at either side. Apply side strips in the same manner. Trim and turn under the ends of the top and bottom strips to form a mitre. Pin.

◫ Turn in the raw edges of the border and the foundation fabric to meet each other round the outside and either topstitch or slipstitch in place. Slipstitch mitres.

◫ Cut four strips of 5.5cm (2¼in) wide ribbon (8) to the length of the centre square and apply them, mitring the corners as with the outer border.

◫ Cut four strips of 1.5cm (⅝in) wide ribbon (9) and apply as shown to the second square, using the same technique.

THE LOG CABIN TABLECLOTH

◫ From the foundation fabric, cut out four 65cm (25in) squares. Mark the centre with tacking stitches, from corner to corner.

◫ Make up each square in the same way: from red fabric, cut one 10cm (4in) square (A), adding 6mm (¼in) seam allowance all round. Pin the fabric square right side up centrally over the foundation square. Handstitch in place along the seamline.

◫ Divide your fabrics into two groups – plains and patterns. Cut the fabrics into strips: take a long ruler and coloured pencil and mark strips 6.2cm (2½in) wide across the fabric width, then cut out.

◫ Take a plain strip (B) and trim to the length of the centre square. Place face down on square, matching edges, and pin and stitch. Fold strip back to the right side. Take a second plain strip (C); trim to length of A plus B and apply in the same way as before.

◫ Continue in the same way, taking the next two strips from the patterned pile and working on round the square. Strips B, C, F and G should be plain, and strips D, E, H and I patterned. After

the last round, tack the free edges to the foundation square.

◫ Join the four squares along the patterned edges, so that the plain sides lie at the corners.

◫ Cut four border strips 144cm (56½in) × 10cm (4in) wide. Lay the top and bottom strips face down on the edge of the patchwork and, still taking a 6mm (¼in) seam allowance, stitch the strips to the patchwork, stopping 6mm (¼in) short of the edge of the patchwork at either side and leaving an equal amount overlapping. Join the two remaining strips in the same way. Mitre the corners.

◫ Make up backing fabric to the same size.

◫ Place patchwork and backing with right sides together and machine round the edges, taking a 1.5cm (⅝in) allowance and leaving an opening for turning. Turn and slipstitch opening.

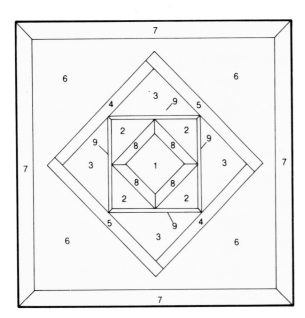

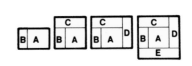

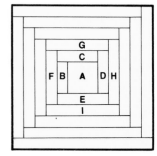

THE OBLONG CUSHION

▦ From fabric cut out the cushion background (1) 63cm × 53cm (24¾in × 21in). Mark the centre both ways with tacking stitches. From fabric cut out the central lozenge (2) with 24cm (9½in) and 20cm (8in) diagonals, adding allowance all round of 6mm (¼in). Place right side up centrally on the background; pin and stitch in place.

▦ Make up a long strip of fabric 150cm × 12.5cm (59in × 5in). Cut a length of 4cm (1½in) wide ribbon to the same length. Place ribbon centrally on right side of fabric strip; pin and stitch in place. From this made-up strip cut four trapeziums (3) with 37cm (14in) and 16cm (6¼in) long edges, plus allowance. Pin and stitch together at diagonal edges. Turn under seam allowance on remaining edges. Pin on background, stitch in place.

▦ From fabric cut out a lozenge (4) with diagonals of 11cm (4¼in) and 9cm (3½in), adding allowance. Turn under allowance and place over centre. Pin and stitch in place.

▦ Apply ribbon (5) round the outer edge of the made-up centre in the same way as for the bed square.

▦ For the four corners (6), from fabric cut out four isosceles

triangles with two 12cm (4¾in) sides, divided by a right angle, adding seam allowances all round. Turn under base edge and place to each corner of background. Pin and stitch in place.

▦ For the cushion back, cut out two pieces of fabric, each 63cm by 28cm (24¼in by 11in). Place backs with right sides together; along one long side, pin and stitch in from outer edges for 15cm (6in), taking 1.5cm (⅝in) seam allowance. Pin and stitch a zip into the central opening. Open zip. Place back to patchwork front with right sides together; pin and stitch all round, taking 1.5cm (⅝in) seam allowance. Turn to right side.

▦ Handstitch cord all round the outer edge of the cushion along the seamline. Stitch a tassel to each corner. Insert cushion pad; close zip.

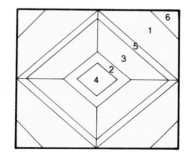

THE OCTAGONAL CUSHION

▦ From fabric cut out a 60cm (23½in) foundation square. Mark the centre both ways with tacking. Cut out a 14cm (5½in) square (1) (plus allowance). Stitch centrally to foundation.

▦ Make up 14cm (5½in) squares (2) (plus allowance) by joining strips of fabric together. In the same way, make up isosceles triangles (3) with 14cm (5½in) long sides, divided by a right angle.

▦ Pin and stitch the squares and triangles together as shown in the diagram. Place this patchwork section over the centred square, hiding the raw edges. Turn under the inner and outer edges; pin and stitch.

▦ Make up the central square (4) from four isosceles triangles with 17cm (6¾in) base and 11.5cm (4½in) sides (plus allowances). Each triangle is made up from rows of ribbon and fabric. Position square 4 diagonally over the centre of square 1; turn under the outer edge; pin and stitch in place.

The complicated effect is achieved by stitching together strips of fabric and ribbon and then stitching the resulting bands together. The exception is the central square where all the seams match.

▦ Trim down foundation square in line with the patchwork. For the surround, cut a length of fabric 160cm × 7cm (63in × 2¾in) plus allowance. Pin and stitch together into a ring. Pin and stitch round the central octagon, making small pleats at each corner, to achieve the correct shape.

▦ For back of cushion cover, cut two pieces to the size of half the patchwork and border, plus a 1.5cm (⅝in) allowance along the long edge. Join along long edge, leaving a 30cm (12in) gap for the zip at the centre. Tack along seam; pin, tack and stitch zip and open.

▦ With right sides together, join cushion back to front and turn out through zip opening.

▦ From plain cotton, make cushion pad to the same size as cover, fill with stuffing and close. Insert pad into cover.

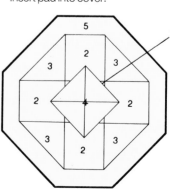

AMERICAN DREAM

The themes used in this charming wall hanging are quintessentially American – block patchwork, album quilts and blue jeans – a visual tribute to the pioneers of the mid-west. Block patterns, so called because the patchwork was divided up into easily manageable blocks, are very characteristic of American work. Sometimes, perhaps to celebrate a wedding, a group of friends and relatives would join together to make an album quilt, like this one: each person would make a different block and then they would meet together and have a party at which the blocks would be joined together and quilted.

Finished size: the work can be as large or as small as you want – or feel you have time for

MATERIALS

Calico and denim fabrics	*Squared graph paper*
Backing fabric	*Card and craft knife*
Light-weight polyester wadding	*Coloured pencils and lead pencil*
or domett	*Matching threads*

METHOD

◼ The patchwork is made up of blocks (sixteen small squares) alternated with plain squares, making five large squares across and down. Blocks normally measure between 20cm (8in) and 36cm (15in) across, so finished piece could measure from 100cm (40in) to 180cm (75in) either way. Each small square, made from two triangles, could therefore measure from 5cm (2in) to 9cm (3¾in) each way.

◼ When you have decided how large you wish the work to be, draw a small square to full scale on graph paper and divide it diagonally into two triangles. Draw up another triangle to the same scale and add 6mm (¼in) seam allowance all round.

◼ Cut out one triangle without allowance and one with, leaving some extra space all round, and stick to card, then cut out along the pencil lines with a craft knife to make two templates.

◼ Using coloured pencils, make a small-scale drawing of the finished work, then use it to work out how many triangles you will need from each fabric. Using the larger template, and a coloured pencil, mark out the appropriate number of patches on each fabric.

◼ Using the smaller template and leaving an even space all round, mark out the inner, sewing line on each patch, then cut out patches. If you are sewing by machine, you need not mark the sewing line as you can use the outer edge of the presser foot as a guide or else stick a length of masking tape on the base plate, 6mm (¼in) away from the needle.

◼ Proceed to arrange the triangles into geometric patterns of your choice or according to the

With triangles as the base, even using only two fabrics – calico and denim – design ideas are endless. When stitching the triangles together to make up the squares, just remember to carefully match up the seams, as *bad joins will spoil the look of the quilt, and the square produced will be off grain. After stitching, press all the seam allowance to one side, before working the next seam.*

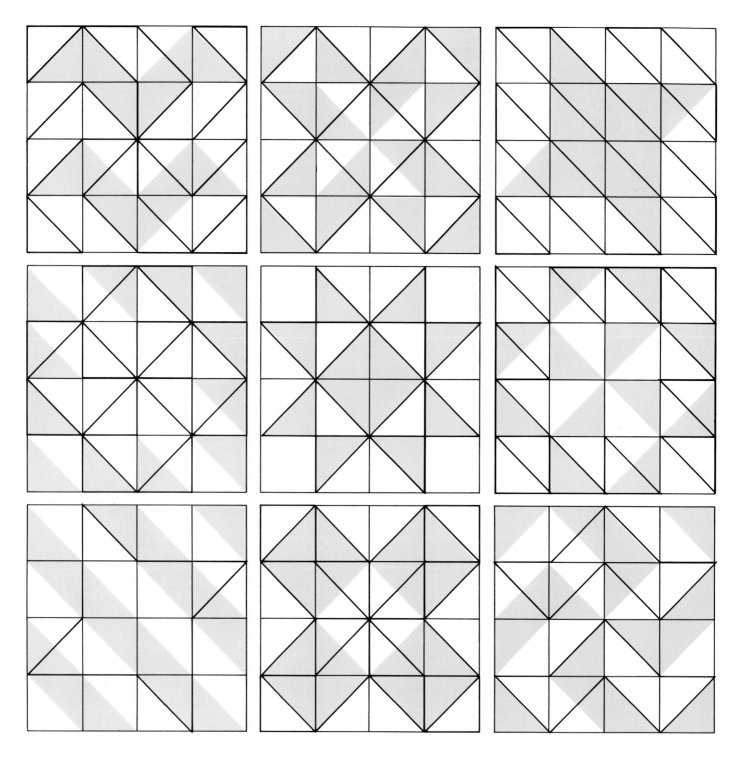

Use these blocks to calculate how much colour you will need in each fabric. Draw each on graph paper and shade in the colours of your choice, then work out the total number of patches in each fabric.

Remembering to add seam allowances, and bearing in mind you can fit two triangles together to make a square, divide the width of your fabric, less selvedges, by the width of a patch, to find out how many patches you can fit across the width of your fabric. Use this to work out the length of fabric required in each colour, adding a small amount for possible mistakes during cutting.

picture. The easiest way to do this is to join the triangles into squares, the squares into rows and the rows into blocks. Join the patches by machine or by hand: if by machine, sew from edge to edge and press seams open, if by hand, sew along the marked line only, using a small running stitch and backstitching at either end, and press seams to one side.

▦ When you have made the patchwork blocks, cut 13 plain squares from calico, to the same size as the blocks. Place blocks and squares flat on a large surface in the correct order, and stitch them together in vertical rows. Join rows to complete the patchwork.

▦ Cut a backing piece and wadding (if you intend to quilt the work) to the size of the finished patchwork. Pin and tack together. If quilting, work running stitch by hand along the lines of the design,

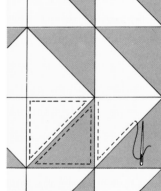

making sure that the needle passes through all layers.

▦ For the border, cut four strips of denim the length of each side plus twice the border width, and seam allowances by twice the border width plus seam allowances.

▦ Mitre the border ends as on page 15: fold each strip in half lengthways and fold in the two corners at either end. Press and cut along creased lines. Place ends with right sides together; pin and stitch to within 1.5cm (⅝in) of edges. Trim and turn to right side, pushing out the mitred corners. Pin and stitch one border edge to hanging; turn under remaining edge and stitch to wrong side.

SEMINOLE PATCHWORK

This intricately patterned patchwork would be the focal point of any room setting: drape it over a bed or table, display it as a wall hanging, or expand the size with extra squares and make a room divider. Although it looks dauntingly complex and difficult to sew, appearances are deceptive, for it is made up by a simple machine technique invented by the Seminole Indians of southern Florida . . . Instead of cutting and sewing each patch separately, the secret is to machine stitch long strips of fabric together – the strips are then cut across and reassembled, producing an elaborate mosaic effect with the minimum of effort.

Finished size: 128cm (50½in) square

MATERIALS

90cm (36in) wide cotton fabric as follows:
1.5m (1⅝yd) in ochre
1m (1yd) in prune
80cm (⅞yd) in brick
70cm (¾yd) in brown
60cm (¾yd) in rose pink
50cm (⅝yd) in beige

10cm (4in) in khaki
1.4m (1½yd) of 137cm (54in) wide cotton fabric, for backing
50cm (⅝yd) of 137cm (54in) wide cotton fabric in blue, for border
Matching threads
Set square
Ruler

METHOD

▦ The patchwork quilt is made up of sixteen squares, each 27cm (10⅝in) in size. Each square has a different arrangement of fabrics, chosen from the seven used for the project.

▦ There are two basic techniques used for the squares. In the first, two fabrics are cut up into equal-width strips. These strips are then stitched together, alternating the two colours. The resulting piece is then cut up into equal-sized strips, the cuts running at right angles to the stripes. This produces new strips, made of patchwork, which are then aligned to form a building brick arrangement, before being stitched together and trimmed to form the final square. This method can also be used with three or four different colours.

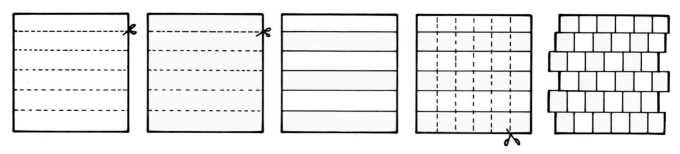

1 Take two or more pieces of fabric and trim them to the same size.

2 Join the strips together taking 6mm (¼in) seams and alternating the colours.

3 Mark lines across the piece of strip patchwork, at right angles to the bands of colour, and cut along the marked lines.

4 Assemble the patchwork strips to make a stepped pattern and join taking 6mm (¼in) seams. Trim uneven edges.

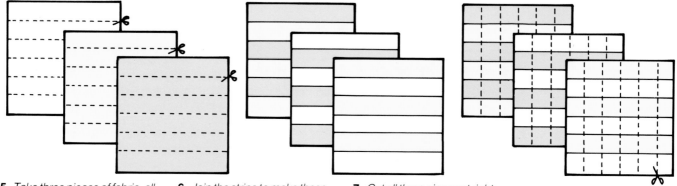

5 Take three pieces of fabric, all the same size, and mark and cut them into strips.

6 Join the strips to make these different two-colour patchwork pieces.

7 Cut all three pieces at right angles to the strips of colour. Assemble the patchwork strips to make a chequer-board pattern.

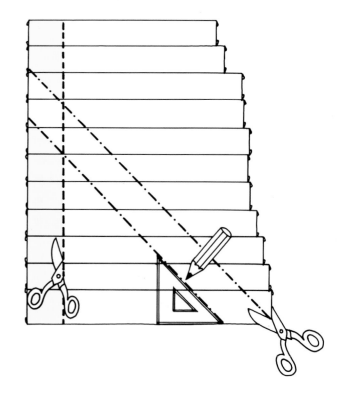

In the second technique, the fabrics are again cut into strips and joined to make a piece of strip patchwork. This time, however, instead of cutting at right angles across the strips, the cuts are made at an angle to produce strips of diamond-shaped patches. Using a set square, mark across the piece of strip patchwork at an angle of 45 degrees either to the left or to the right. In each case the strips of patchwork are aligned to achieve a diagonal effect. The two strips with the patches running in opposite directions can be joined together to create a chevron effect.

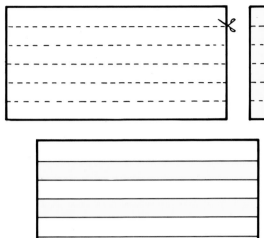

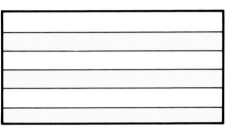

1 *For diamond and chevron patterns, take two fabrics. Press them and trim away any selvedges. Mark both fabrics in strips of equal width. Cut along the lines and then join the strips together, alternating the colours and taking 6mm (¼in) seam allowances.*

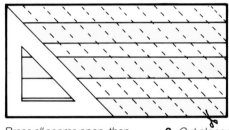

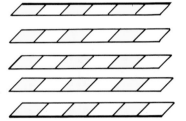

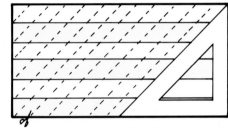

2 *Press all seams open, then mark off strips at an angle of 45° to the previous ones.*

3 *Cut along the marked lines and pile them up, maintaining the colour order.*

4 *For a chevron pattern, make up a second, identical piece of straight-strip patchwork, then*

mark it with strips angled to the right (assuming that the first strips angled leftwards).

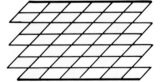

5 *Cut along the strips of second piece, keeping them separate from the first pile.*

6 *The bands from the second piece of patchwork can form left-leaning diamonds.*

7 *The bands from the first piece make right-leaning diamonds, as in square J.*

8 *Bands from both pieces alternate to form a chevron pattern.*

Following these two techniques make up the squares in the following way. Remember to add 6cm (¼in) seam allowance to the strip measurements and cut all strips 45cm (22in) long.

A – Use technique 1 in prune and pink. Cut out 4.5cm (1¾in) wide strips of fabric each time.

B – Use technique 2 in prune and ochre. Cut out 3cm (1¼in) wide strips, then cut diagonally to the right, making 5.5cm (2¼in) wide bands.

C – Use technique 1 in ochre, beige and pink. Cut out 3cm (1¼in) wide strips each time.

D – Use technique 2 in prune and brick. Cut out 3cm (1¼in) wide strips, then cut a mixture of left and right diagonal strips into 4cm (1¼in) wide bands.

E – Make up this square in the same way, in prune and brown, as square D, but cutting 5.5cm (2¼in) wide bands.

F – Make up this square in the same way, in ochre and brick, as square D, but cut out 2cm (¾in) wide strips and make up 6cm (2¼in) wide bands.

G – Make up this square in the same way, in ochre and brown, as square D, but cut out 4.5cm (1¾in) wide strips and make up 6cm (2¼in) wide bands.

H – Make up this square in the same way, in pink and beige, as square D, but cut out 3.5cm (1¼in) wide strips and make up into 5cm (2in) wide bands.

I – For this square use technique 1, in beige and ochre. Cut out 2.5cm (1in) wide strips each time.

J – For this square use technique 2, in brick and prune. Cut out 3.5cm (1¼in) wide strips, then cut diagonally to the left into 5.5cm (2¼in) wide bands.

K – Use technique 1 for this square in prune, khaki, pink and brown. Cut out 4cm (1½in) wide strips each time.

L – Make up this square in the same way, in ochre and prune, as square J, but cut out 4.5cm (1¾in) wide strips each time.

M – Make up this square in the same way in pink and beige, as square D, but cut out 2.5cm (1in) wide strips and make up into 4.5cm (1¾in) wide bands.

N – Make up this square in the same way, in ochre and brown, as square D, but cut out 3cm (1¼in) wide strips and make them up into 6cm (2¼in) wide bands.

O – Make up this square in the same way, in prune and brown, as square D, but cut out 2.5cm (1in) wide strips and make up 5.5cm (2¼in) wide bands.

P – Make up this square in the same way, in ochre and brick, as square D, but cut out 1.5cm (⅝in) wide strips and make them up into 5.5cm (2¼in) wide bands.

When all the squares are complete, pin and stitch them together in the correct order, following the diagram, with right sides together and taking 6mm (¼in) wide seam allowances.

For the border, cut out two strips of blue fabric, each 109cm × 12cm (43in × 4¾in) for top and bottom of quilt. Place each strip with right side to patchwork; pin and stitch, taking 6mm (¼in) seam allowances. Fold down the border strips with right sides up. From blue fabric cut out two strips, each 131cm × 12cm (51½in × 4¾in) for sides. Position each strip to the remaining sides of the patchwork, with right sides together. Pin and stitch in place. Fold down the border strips with right sides up.

From backing fabric cut out one piece 137cm (54in) square. Place to patchwork with wrong sides together; pin and tack all round. Turn 3cm (1¼in) wide border of backing fabric over to the right side of the quilt; turn under 6mm (¼in). Stitch in place.

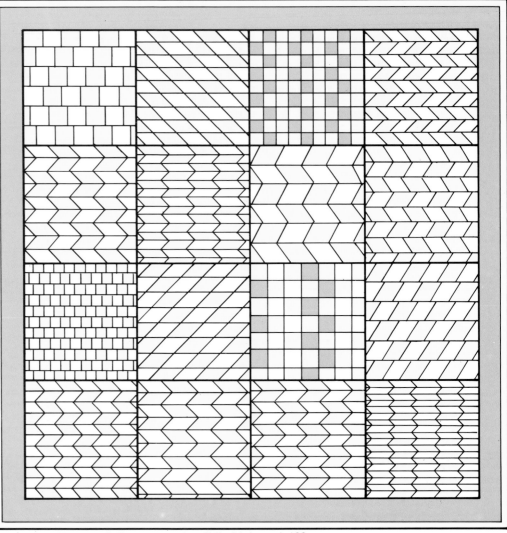

A	B	C	D
E	F	G	H
I	J	K	L
M	N	O	P

After making up each individual square, stitch them together in the above order to achieve the quilt.

WHITE AS SNOW

Designed for a gleaming Scandinavian home, all white from cellar to attic, this unusual and elegant cover is decorated with interlaced bands of white leather which provide a subtle and sophisticated contrast with the cellular warmth and soft texture of the background. Use the blanket as a lightweight summer cover or snuggle under it for extra warmth in winter as you drink your ice-cold aquavit.

Size: 140cm×140cm (55in×55in).

MATERIALS

1.4m (1½yd) of 140cm (55in) wide cellular blanket fabric or an old single blanket or two or more cot blankets joined or 25 knitted or crocheted squares each measuring 28cm×28cm (11in×11in),

joined together to make one large square Two white lambskins (sufficient to make up strips as listed below) or 50cm (⅝yd) of 140cm (55in) wide leather-type fabric Matching thread

METHOD

▦ If you are making up the 140cm (55in) square from smaller 28cm (11in) squares, first make the squares, knitting or crocheting them, or cutting up blanketing to size. Neaten the edges with zigzag stitch, then lay the pieces side by side and

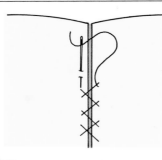

herringbone stitch across the joins. Join on one side first, then turn the work over and join the pieces on the other side. Press lightly.

▦ Cut leather into strips as follows, joining pieces as necessary to achieve the correct length: one strip 560cm×6cm (220in×2½in) and eight strips 146cm×3cm (57⅛in×1¼in).

▦ Fold the long strip in half lengthwise, with right sides together, and place it over the edge of the blanket, with the edge of the blanket against the inner fold edge of the strip. Hold in place with paper clips. Fold each corner into a mitre and position the ends of the strip so that they will be covered by one of the strips laid across the blanket.

▦ Remove strip from blanket and stitch corner mitres. Trim and press seams open, then turn strip right side out and once again clip around edge of blanket. Topstitch in position, close to the edges of the leather.

▦ Lay the blanket flat and position four 3cm (1¼in) wide strips across it at intervals of 28cm (11in), covering the joined edges of any squares (if necessary). The 3cm (1¼in) extra length at each end is brought round to the back of the blanket. Lay the remaining four strips across, interweaving them with the first as shown in the diagram. The strips are topstitched to the blanket down both edges, so place any essential pins along the future lines of stitching, to avoid marking the leather.

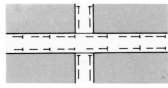

▦ The strips must be sewn in position one by one. Note where subsequent strips will lie over the strip which is being sewn and hold these strips clear of the stitching, pinning them back in position after the stitching is complete, so that the finished lines of stitching follow the interwoven pattern.

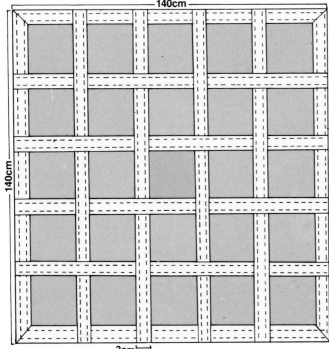

CUBIST THROW

If your friends think that patchwork is all tiny scraps stitched in regular patterns, startle them with this restrained but beautiful sofa throw based on a picture by Braque. The muted shades overlap against a plain background, and the clearly defined borders give the effect of a picture frame. Although we suggest how to make the borders, the size, colouring and placement of the patches is up to you – this is your own work of art.

Finished size: approximately 130cm (51in) square

MATERIALS

120cm (48in) wide brushed cotton as follows:
1.2m (1⅓yd) cream
1m (1¼yd) brown
70cm (¾yd) dark brown

50cm (⅝yd) beige
Oddments of brown, beige, rust and grey plain and patterned brushed cotton fabrics
Matching threads

METHOD

▦ Cut out one 96cm (37½in) square of brown fabric and centre it on the cream square. Pin, tack and zigzag stitch in place.

▦ From beige fabric, cut four strips, each 111cm × 6cm (44in × 2½in). Mark two lines by tacking all round the cream square 4.5cm (2in) and 10.5cm (4½in) from the outer edge, making sure that the stitching is parallel with the edge.

▦ Tack the first beige strip between tacked lines. Lay next strip with right sides together over first strip. At the corner, stitch diagonally through all layers of fabric from inner to outer corner. Turn second strip back to lie along second edge of throw and tack.

▦ Work each corner in the same way, until the last corner: turn under the last end on the diagonal and crease. Place over the first end and stitch together along creased line. Zigzag stitch all the strips in place along both edges.

▦ Cut out rectangles of rust and beige fabrics each 6cm × 3cm (2½in × 1¼in) and alternate them along the outer edge of the beige border, leaving spaces the same size in between. Pin, tack and zigzag in position.

▦ From a variety of plain and patterned fabrics cut out squares of assorted sizes, from about

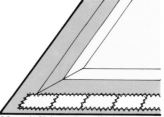

30cm (12in) to 15cm (6in). Lay the squares in a haphazard fashion over the central brown square, sometimes overlapping. Pin and zigzag stitch each layer in place.

▦ For outer edges, make up four strips of dark brown fabric each 127cm × 13cm (50½in x 5½in). Fold each strip in half lengthways. At the ends, bring up short edges to fold and press. Cut along creased line. Unfold. Pin, tack and stitch short edges of strips together, along mitred angle, leaving

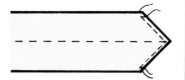

1.5cm (⅝in) unstitched at outer edges. Trim and turn corner to right side, making a mitre. Turn under 1.5cm (⅝in) all round inner edges; slide mitred border over the edge of the work to meet the oblong strip border. Pin, tack and topstitch.

PATCHWORK CURTAIN

Sunlight filtering through a white cotton curtain, illuminating patches of chintz scattered with flowers, birds or butterflies, like little scenes in a stained glass window – what could be prettier? Some patchwork techniques can be rather time consuming, but here is a way of achieving the charm and character of a traditional patchwork by using a very quick and easy machine method. Drape the finished piece over a pole or make it into a conventional curtain.

Size: to fit your own requirements.

MATERIALS

Plain white cotton fabric to
    desired size
Assortment of floral-patterned
    cotton fabrics for appliqué

Matching threads
Pair of sharp-pointed embroidery
    scissors

METHOD

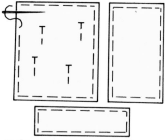

▦ Decide on the finished size of the curtain and cut out one piece of plain white cotton fabric to this size, adding 4cm (1½in) on the width and 14cm (5¾in) to the length for hem and top.

▦ Turn under a double 1cm (⅜in) hem on both side edges. Turn under a double 6cm (2½in) hem on base edge, making neat base corners. Pin, tack and stitch all round. Turn under and stitch a double 1cm (⅜in) hem along top edge.

▦ Press the curtain to eliminate all the creases and lay flat on a large work surface right side up.

▦ From the chosen appliqué fabrics cut out squares and rectangles in different sizes, ranging from about 7.5cm (3in) to 25cm (10in) either way. In some cases two or more fabrics can be stitched together with plain flat seams to form multi-coloured sections. Mark, then cut out each piece, allowing for a margin all around of about 2cm (¾in).

▦ Position all the appliqué pieces right side up on the right side of the curtain and move them about until the desired effect is reached, then pin and tack in place. Vertically tack large pieces to the background to keep them flat.

▦ Straight stitch round each piece along the marked outline and fasten off securely. Using a pair of sharp-pointed embroidery scissors, cut away the allowance from around each piece very close to the stitching line. Take care not to cut through the stitches.

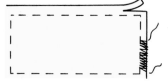

▦ Set the sewing-machine to a zigzag stitch. Before stitching, test the stitch on a spare piece of fabric and adjust the stitch size if necessary. Stitch round each piece in turn. After stitching pull all the working threads through to the wrong side and fasten off. Remove the tacking stitches and press.

▦ Hang the curtain draped over a curtain pole beside the bed.

TWEED BLANKET

Irish tweeds provide a rich and unusual patchwork fabric. This luxuriously warm blanket, with its warm blend of natural, earthy colours, would look equally at home in a country cottage or an ultra-modern setting. Although these heavier fabrics are not as easy to make up into patchwork as the more commonly used cottons, there is no great difficulty in joining these large-scale uncomplicated patches. If you don't want to buy the tweeds, use jumble sale finds (if the fabric is still in good condition) or ask tailoring shops if you can have their outdated sample books.

Finished size: the blanket can be as large or as small as you desire

MATERIALS

An assortment of different coloured tweed fabrics
Piece of flannelette sheeting or cotton domett for interlining

Piece of tweed or heavy brushed cotton the finished size for backing and the borders
Matching threads

METHOD

▢ Cut out a 15cm (6in) square template from card, making sure that each corner is a right angle. Using this template mark and cut out squares from each of the tweed fabrics, allowing a 1cm (⅜in) seam allowance all round.
▢ Lay all the squares out on the floor and move them about until you have the desired effect, then pile them up in order in rows. Number rows by pinning a piece of paper to the top of each pile.
▢ Begin by joining the squares together to form widthways rows: place the first two squares with right sides together; pin, tack and stitch. Repeat to stitch all the squares together to complete the first row. Trim and press seams open. Repeat for each row.
▢ Place the first two rows with right sides together; pin, tack and stitch together, making sure that the seams match. Repeat, until one half of the patchwork is made, then join up the other half. Finish by sewing the two halves together.
▢ Cut and join sheeting or domett, if using, and tweed backing to the size of the finished patchwork plus an extra 8.5cm (3¼in) all round. Lay the sheeting on the wrong side of the backing: pin, tack and stitch, using an ordinary running stitch and sewing 1.5cm (⅝in) from the raw edges.
▢ Centre the patchwork over the sheeting and, in the same way, pin, tack and stitch all round, 1.5cm (⅝in) in from edge of the patchwork.
▢ For a border, cut two strips of tweed 23cm (9in) wide to the length of the blanket backing plus 3cm (1¼in) and two to the width plus 3cm (1¼in). At the end of each strip, bring the corners together, forming a mitre, as on page 15. Press, then cut along pressed lines.
▢ Place strips together in order: pin, tack and stitch across shaped ends to within 1.5cm (⅝in) of edges. Press seams open.
▢ Place border frame to right side of patchwork: pin, tack and stitch.
▢ Fold border over to enclose all raw edges and slipstich in position at the back.

ACKNOWLEDGMENTS

2 M. Duffas/J. Schoumacher
5 G. de Chabaneix/I. Garçon
6 M. Duffas/J. Schoumacher
7 P. Hussenot/J. Schoumacher
8 G. de Chabaneix/
C. de Chabaneix/Jacobs
9 A. Bianchi/I. Garçon
11 G. de Chabaneix/
J. Schoumacher
12-23 above left M. Duffas/
J. Schoumacher
23 above right and below
P. Hussenot/J. Schoumacher
25-37 M. Duffas/J. Schoumacher
38-39 B. Maltaverne/C. Lebeau
41 Y. Duronsoy/Jacobs
43-44 J. Laiter/I. Garçon
46 P. Hussenot/J. Schoumacher
48 B. Maltaverne/C. Lebeau
51 M. Garçon/J. Schoumacher

52 above M. Duffas/
J. Schoumacher
52 below, 53 M. Garçon/
J. Schoumacher
55 M. Duffas/J. Schoumacher
57 B. Maltaverne/C. Lebeau
60-61 P. Hussenot/
J. Schoumacher
63-67 M. Duffas/J. Schoumacher
68-71 G. Bouchet/C. Lebeau
73-75 G. de Chabaneix/
C.Lebeau
77 G. de Chabaneix/
C. de Chabaneix
81-82 Maclean/C. Lebeau/
J. Schoumacher
84 G. de Chabaneix/
C. de Chabaneix/Jacobs
86 M. Duffas/J. Schoumacher
89 G. de Chabaneix/

J. Schoumacher
93-94 B. Maltaverne/C. Lebeau
97 J. Dirand/C. Lebeau
100-103 M. Duffas/
J. Schoumacher
107 Godeaut/C. Lebeau
111-113 G. de Chabaneix/
C. de Chabaneix/Jacobs
114 A. Bianchi/I. Garçon
116-121 G. de Chabaneix/
I. Garçon
123-125 B. Maltaverne/
C. Lebeau
126-129 G. de Chabaneix/
I. Garçon
130-135 A. Bianchi/I. Garçon
137-139 M. Duffas/
J. Schoumacher
141 N. Bruant/C. Lebeau
142-143 B. Maltaverne/C. Lebeau